T0381163

IRAQ

Emil Tzolov

Order this book online at www.trafford.com
or email orders@trafford.com

Most Trafford titles are also available at major online book retailers.

Print information available on the last page.

ISBN: 978-1-6987-0776-1 (sc)
ISBN: 978-1-6987-0777-8 (e)

Trafford rev. 06/03/2021

www.trafford.com

North America & international
toll-free: 844-688-6899 (USA & Canada)
fax: 812 355 4082

War is only waste of lives :
Confutius, 543 B.C.

Who plays gulf will
die at the Gulf!
German pacifist proverb

14-11-2001

In Kunduz the Northern Alliance encircled 20000 Taliban fighters from Pakistan, Chechnya, Egypt and Dagestan. An UN food convoy had reached its destination in Afghanistan, said UN in Geneva. Till now the Taliban have lost 12 provinces but still posses 31 further provinces. The Northern Alliance has not full control over the country said the German Intelligence Service, which expects the Taliban to fall back to guerilla tactics. US defence Secretary Donald Rumsfeld said there were fierce fightinga in and around the Southern city of Kandahar-a stronghold of the Taliban.

As the Northern Alliance consolidates its position in the Capital Kabul the situation in crucial Eastern provinces remains fluid. There is report that the former Mujaheddin group had taken the Eastern town of Jalalabad which used to be a Taliban stronghold. Pashawa-based ex-Mujaheddin commanders were trying to restore their authority in the East say they are poised to re-enter the country and assume control but local officials say local uprising has ended Taliban rule in the East. The Pakistan Army and extra border guards are on duty after reports large numbers of Taliban fighters and foreign Islamic militatnts were trying to cross into the lawless tribal areas across the border from Afghanistan.

Pakistani newspapers said the Taliban are planed to conduct a guerilla campaign from bases in the tribal areas. Official in Pakistan said they won't allow that. Kabul remains calm after the arrival of the Northern Alliance troops with the streets full of people and the shopping basars busy. There were guards outsides all goverment buildings and troops were manning main road interseptions. Music which was banned as unislamic under the Taliban rule can once again be heard in the city. Radio Afghanistan was broadcasting again and the female presenters sacked by the Taliban had returned to work. There were long queus at barber shops as men lined up to have threir beards trimmed but women were still wearing their all-enveloping clothing. The Northern Alliance has entranched its position as the only power in the Capital.

Despite of the dramatic events of the few days the British Prime minister Tony Blair said there is still a lot of work to be done before the work of the international coalition against the Taliban was completed: " We still have to make sure that Afghanistan cannot be used to export terrorism round the world; that the al Qaida terrorist network is shut down and that Osama ben Laden and his associates were brought to justice"

Tony Blair said also there was a diplomatic challenge to create a broad-based goverment to take over from the Taliban and there will be a conserted effort to make sure tha humanitarian aid was distributed.

The UN Security Council was meeting to consider a resolution endorsing a plan for a broad based transitional government in Afghanistan. The plan was been drawn up by the UN special envoy Lakhta Brahimi who hopes to organize a meeting of all Afghan factions within a week. This indicates that the UN continue its efforts to find a future settlement in Afghanistan.

Later in the day Afghan refugees and aid workers said that the Taliban still hold the key Southern city of Kandahar but their position was becoming increasingly fragile. At the border point of Chaman Taliban soldiers and refugees from Kandahar were crossing into Pakistan.

The border crossing point at Chaman was extremely tense. The BBC correspondent there Adam Brooks saw Taliban fighters and frightened refugees making their way into Pakistan. The Taliban were keen to persuade the BBC that in Kandahar-the city that controls Southern Afghanistan-their commrades are still entranched and ready to fight but refugees told a different story. They said there were noticebly fewer Taliban in the city than in previous weeks and a group of aid workers who had left Kandahar only hours previously said moral among Taliban fighters was low and several of their commanders had left the city to seek refuge in the surrounding mountains. The picture is very confused but reports from the border suggest that the Taliban grip on the city was starting to erode. Reprorts were coming in that Taliban started to lose control in provinces all over Afghanistan allthough not exclusively to the opposition Northern Alliance. Councils of tribal Elders who oppose the Alliance said they controlled various provinces in the East of the country. Several were calling for the return of the former King of Afghanistan Zahir Shah. One of the leading factions in the Alliance-the Jamati Islami-took power on 13 Nov in the Afghan Capital Kabul from where the BBC correspondent Kate Clark said at 17:00 GMT most of Afghanistan had fallen under the control of the anti-Taliban forces but they come from different parties, tribes and ethnic groups. In the East 5 provinces appeared to be ruled by tribal Elders who opposed the Northern Alliance. One of them-Jamah Ath-took control of Kabul on 13 Nov. The Elders were calling for the return of the former King of Afghanistan. The Capital Kabul was calm with Jamah Ath police patroling the streets. The Jamah Ath leader Buhanadin Rabani is due to fly from Tajikistan in a deeply symbolic act. At least one more member of the Northern Alliance had already set up defensive position in the West of Kabul. As Taliban central control unravels Afghanistan was fragmenting. Heavy fighting was reported from the town of Kunduz; there were no signs that the Taliban were going to lay down their arms;there some 20000 foreign fighters in the town which is on the strategic road linking the Tajik and the Afghan capitals. Reports from Jalalabad said the city had fallen to the Northern Alliance but no one could confirm this. The city of Kandahar remained firmly in the hands of the Taliban. Mula Muhammad Omar-the Taliban supreme leader-phoned up the BBC and told the Pashtoon service that they are firmly in control of Kandahar; if necessary they will fight on from the surrounding mountains. The Taliban had a big plan Mula Omar said but declined to elaborate.

The faith of Kandahar remained uncertain. The British Prime minister Tony Blar said British troops were set on 48 hours notice and he did not exclude the posibility of engaging British troops in Afghanistan while at 21:00 GMT American special troops were already operating in Kabul.

15-11-2001

A senior Pashtoon leader in opposition to the Taliban said a heavy fighting contunued around the spiritual Taliban stronghold in the South city of Kandahar. The leader-Hamed Kharzy-said there was a popular uprising in the area against the Taliban who were withdrawing heavy equipment from the city. There was no independent confirmation of this. Taliban sources in the Pakistani city of Quetta said the Taliban were withdrawing from the Central Afghan province of Guzny but aid agencies said key South city of Kandahar remained in Taliban hands. Guzny lyes halfway between Kabul and the Southern Taliban stronghold of Kandahar. It is strategically signifficant because it stradles the main Kabul-Kandaahar highway.

It was not clear whether the pull-out was an organized withdrawal or the Taliban had simply collapsed but it means that another large suade of Afghanistan might lack any recognisable political control. Aid agencies said that the key Southern city of Kandahar remained in Taliban hands; relief workers in the city confirmed that Taliban fighters were still in evidence on the streets but one aid agency's spokesman described the situation there as "confused and fluctuating", said the BBC correspondent in the area Adam Brooks.

Taliban troops led by Arab and Pakistani fighters were reported to put fierce resistence to Northern Alliance forces around the Northern Afghan city of Kunduz. From nearby Talokan BBC correspondent Rupert Winfried Haze reported: "After a week of stunting advances in which after city had fallen with hardly a fight Northern Alliance forces now appear to be facing a real struggle! Along the dusty road between Talokan and Kunduz columns of Northern Alliance troops could be seen moving towards the front. Heavy armour including new tanks supplied by Russia were sent in to try dislodge Taliban from its last stronghold in the North of the country. But after 4 days of fighting Northern Alliance forces were still too nervous to allow foreign journalists to visit the front. There were even reports that Alliance's forces were pushed back towards Talokan". The UN deputy representative to Afghanistan Fracesk Vendrel told the BBC he will go to Afghan Capital Kabul very shortly as part of efforts to convene the council of Afghan groups aimed at setting up of broad-based transitional goverment. He said he was confident that the Northern Alliance would cooperate fully with efforts to form a Goverment in Afghanistan. He said the former King had a great role to play.

He told the BBC that the UN aimed to start with small presence in Kabul and will expand its operations as conditions improve. He said that the Northern Alliance which controlled Kabul had consistently indicated that it was of favour of relinquishing power to a broad-based goverment. Meanwhile the US-envoy to Afghanistan James Dobbin was holding talks in Pakistan on the plans of transitional goverment. He arrived from Rom where he met the former King of Afghanistan Zahir Shah. The King himself made a pre-recorded speech for the Ramadan celebration saying he wanted to return to Afghanistan but not as a ruler but as an ordinary citizen serving his country. 8 aid workers who were detained by the Taliban on charges of preaching Christianity were brought out of Afghanistan by American special forces. Pres. Bush said it was an incredibly good news. The 2 Americans, 2 Australians and 4 Germans were arrested 3.5 months ago along with 16 Afghans. American officials said their 3 helicopters picked up the 8 aid workers in a high risc operation from a field South from Kabul. They were flown to Islamabad's military airport and than to their respecting Embassies. The operation began after a local military commander in Guzny-province contacted the international Red Cross saying he had the foreign aid workers and wanted assistence to get them out. The Taliban said this was one of their commanders; he called the Red Cross because he feared the aid workers could be killed. The Taliban deputy representative in Islamabad Zaher Shahin said not a single bullit was fired, reported the BBC correspondent Suzanne Price from Islamabad.

Western aid workers said the Taliban lost control over Jalalabad and it was now in the hands of local anti-Taliban militia. Pakistan increased control over its frontier with Afghanistan;armoured vehicles, tanks and troops arrived at at the border town of Chaman and check points established at key border crossing points.

Officials were concerned that refugees and fighters from Afghanistan might try to cross into Pakistan Anti-Taliban forces had captured also the town of Tarrin Kowt-native town of the Taliban spiritual leader Mula Omar. A top American military official was visiting Kabul to access humanitarian needs there. At the Pentagon the American Defence Secretary Donald Rumsfeld said Osama ben Laden might try to slip out of Afghanistan while the American Commander for Afghanistan General Tomy Francs stated the hour was coming when Osama ben Laden and his al Qaida associates would be cought;this was only a matter of time. 1OO British troops arrived at the Bagram airport in Kabul at 21:44 GMT.

Crown Prince Abdulah of Saudi Arabia urged the country's senior Islamic clerics to exercise caution in their public statements saying they had responsibility towards their faith and goverments. The Crownprince told the clerics that Saudi Arabia was going through difficult times and they should not allowed themselves to be swept away by emotions China released information which links ethnic Wiga separatists in the North-West province of Shin-Xiang to international terrorist networks;a foreign ministry's spokesman said several hundreds Wiga separatists were trained in Afghan camps linked to Osama ben Laden. He also named several groups responsible for attacks in Shin-Xiang in the 199Oies and the bombing of the Chinese Consulate in Istambul in 1998.

16-11-2001

Begin of the Muslim holy month of Ramadan;Pres. Bush congratulated the Muslim world and its desire for peace.

At 12:37 GMT Alex Prody said in BBC-newshour: "I cannot understand is there(in Afghanistan) crisis or is it no crisis?"

Elite British troops secured the Bagram airport 25 km North of Kabul;Bagram has the longest runway in Afghanistan.

Their mission is to prepare the airport for flights and for possible arrival of furhter miliatary forces. The British goverment said Bagram would be used for humanitarian operations. But the food aid need in Afghanistan requires truck convoys rather rather than planes coming into a single airport. The British goverment could have other unstated aims and the Northern Alliance troops in Kabul were uneasy at the British presence, said the BBC reporter in Kabul Kate Clark.

The Capital Kabul is held only by one faction of the Northern Alliance-the Tajic Jamati Islamia-while further factions press for a large international presence. Their spokesman said they were not consulted about the arrival of the British troops. The BBC correspondent in Kabul there were mixed feelings about their presence in Kabul. But elements within the leadership of the Northern Alliance in Kabul were uneasy about their arrival esp. if pre-satges larger missions.

Russia sent govermental delegation to Afghanistan for talks with the "legitimate goverment of Afghanistan" which comes to imply that Russia supports the Northern Alliance rather than the former King. Announcing the move the defence minister Sergey Ivanov said the mission would include representatives of the ministries of foreign affairs, defence and emergencies. The delegations was due due to meet representatives of the "lawful goverment in Afghanistan" The BBC Moscow correspondent Steve Rozenberg said this was a clear referrence to Northern Alliance which Russia had continued to recognize as legitimate administration of Afghanistan throughout the years of Taliban supremacy.

American planes carried out further heavy bombing raids on the Taliban Southern stronghold of Kandahar. The Afghan Islamic Press Agency said that the Taliban foreign ministry was hit, a mosque was destroyed and a number of civilians killed. Ethnic Pashtoon leaders in Pakistan said Taliban forces were rapidly building new defensive positions in Kandahar. In a BBC from Kandahar Muhammad Tayab Aga-spokesman for Mula Muhammad Omar-said the Taliban will not give up the city but the leadership was considering pleads by local tribal groups for the city to be handed over peacefully.

In the Eastern city of Jalalabad local militia commanders were discussing the appointment of a new governor following the departure of the Taliban but they failed sofar to reach an agreement on how to share power. A BBC correspondent in Jalalabad said there was an increasing concern among residents over the failure of the representatives of different factions to reach agreement. There were hundreds of heavily armed gunmen in the streets and it is feared shooting may errupt if talks break down. Some militia commanders had already established road blocks in areas they control. BBC correspondent said those involved in the meeting described it as one "of high stakes" as they have to find agreement not only on governor of Jalalbad but also of all the provinces in Eastern Afghanistan. Thousands of Taliban including many foreign volunteers remained entranched in the Northern city of Kunduz. In Mazar-e Sharif the Northern Alliance continued executing surrendered Taliban fighters.

As Taliban rule weakens there were fears that Afghanistan was rapidly disintegrating into a patchwork of war lords fifdoms; local leaders were taking control in the areas they ruled before the Taliban appeared and imposed a rough unity on the country. The Capital Kabul is held by soldiers from just one faction of the Northern Alliance-the ethnic Tajics of Jamati Islami;they said there was no need for international peace keepers. The international aid agency Oxfam called for an immediate food aid for Afghanistan because thousands of people could be dying from lack of food following the worst draught in living memory. Germany is about to send 4000 German troops into Afghanistan;the German Chancellor Gerhard Schroeder had narowly survived a vote of confidence in the Parliament at the end of the debate on the plans to deploy German troops in Afghanistan. The vote was 336 "for" to 326 "against". The majority of 10 in the vote on which it staked the future of Schroeder's social-democrate green-red coalition.

The plans to deploy 4OOO German troops had lead to a descend within the coalition;Gerhard Schroeder survived after 8 Green MP's opposed to the deployment decided to split their votes so as not to bring DOWN their goverment. The issue had not gone away;opposition to the troops deployment is likely to surface again when the Greens held party conference next weekend. Than they can try to topple their own leadership by passing anti-war resolution. Japan was also preparing troops to send in for logistical support in Afghanistan. French troops had arrived already in Afghanistan.

The US defence secretary Donald Rumsfeld said Americcan special forces were active in Afghanistan shooting Taliban forces who did not surrender and members of the al Qaida network moving around the country. Donald Rumsfeld said there were hundreds of American troops on the ground. Donald Rumsfeld revealed that American troops in Afghanistan had moved beyond the liaison of targetting and supply role which was previously ascribed to them. Brandishing photos of US special forces in Afghanistan : American troops were killing Taliban who would not surrender and mmebers of the al Qaida net work trying to move about the country. At times American forces have been OVERRUN, Donald Rumsfeld said, and air strikes have been called up to provide air support. The leadership of the Taliban and al Qaida are the focus of the US attention.

"They bob and weave and move, the defence secretary said but we are clearly reducing the square mile of geography that they have to function in", reported the BBC correspondent in Washington Johnnie Diamond. Meanwhiles the Pentagon said the bombing of targets in Afghanistan had continued despite the start of the Muslim holy month of Ramadan. The Americans said they have killed in the air raids the second person after Osama ben Laden -Muhammad Atef(?) who was designted to succed Osama ben Laden if he was killed in the battles. He was distinguished military commander.

Muhammad Atef was initially pronounced dead in the suicidal plane attack on the World Trade Center in New York on 11ᵗʰ Sept 2OO1 but it seems now not to be so. Muhammad Atef was described by CNN and by BBC as Taliban Chief of staff. His pronunciation dead took a great pride to the Americans. Later this day Mula Omar agreed to leave peacefully Kandahar and to give over the pover to Mula Nagib and Hadgi-2 Pashtoon tribal leaders described as former Mujaheddin. The US said it does not belive the reports.

17-11-2OO1

The Afghan President deposed by the Taliban 5 years ago Buhanadin Rabani returned to Kabul and promised that his Northern Alliance would not cling to power. Speaking at a news conference in the Capital Prof. Rabani said he would welcome a broad based goverment in Afghanistan as soon as possible. The Northern Alliance would respect the will of the traditional loyal Djerga or Grand Assembly of tribal Elders or faction Chiefs to decide on the future administration. The UN deputy envoy Francesc Vendrel also arrived in Afghanistan to open diplomatic moves on the future of the country. Correspondent said the lightening military advances of the Northern Alliance had left politicians and diplomates crambling to establish a new goverment. A spokesman for the faction of the Northern Alliance which controls Kabul demanded the withdrawal of the British troops deployed at the startegic air base to the North of the city. The spokesman of the Jamiati Islami said that just 15 of the 1OO or so (!) British soldiers at Bagram could stay. He said they were deployed without consultation. A British Goverment spokesman said the British troops at Bagram were discussing the situation with the local commanders. The British said they were securing the air base to bring in humanitarian supplies. Jamiat troops went into Kabul on 13 Nov despite assurances they would hault their advance on the Taliban at the outskirts of the city. The BBC correspondent in Kabul said ordinary Afghans welcome the security of international(=British) military presence there (?). A spokesman of the Taliban leadership in Kandahar Muhammad Talib Aga said the Taliban had no intention of abandoning the city and will continue to defend it. He said that any information to the contrary amounted to Western propaganda. In BBC interview from Kandahar Muhammad Taib Aga said that bombing had continued around the city. There was no fighting and the Taliban leader Mula Mohamed Omar was still in the area under their control. Across the border in Pakistan a Taliban official in the town of Quetta denied earlier reports that a deal was made to hand over Kandahar to 2 former Mujaheddin commanders. Thousands of Taliban soldiers trapped in the Northern Afghan town of Kunduz have been exchanging artillery and rocket fire with the Northern Alliance units surrounding them. The Mayor of Kunduz asked the Northern Alliance troops to delay any advance while he negotiated with the Taliban. The dead line for their surrender runs up on 17 Nov. Kunduz strattles a strategically important road between Tajikistan and Kabul. Many of the Taliban fighters trapped there were foreign volunteers-Arabs, Pakistanis, Chechens and Indonesians. A Taliban official confirmed that a senior Taliban commander Muhammed Atef was killed in an American bombing raid on 14th Nov 2ooo1. The official did not say where the raid took place. At 16:o4 GMT BBC broadcasted a statement of the Taliban envoy to Pakistan Abdul Slam Zaif that Osama ben Laden had fled Afghanistan with his Family. The Americans (?) countered they had no evidence to believe that this was true.

18-11-2001

American aircraft have been intensifying their bombing raids around the Northern Afghan town of Kunduz-the last Northern stronghold of Taliban forces. Witnesses said planes attacked Taliban positions in hills close to Hanabad about 2O km from Kunduz. Northern Alliance commanders whose troops surround Kunduz said they tried to negotiate a peaceful surrender but time was running out. They said they would attack unless Taliban give themselves up today.

If that happens the fight is likely to be bloody;several thousends highly comitted foreign volunteers were in Kunduz and they were more likely than their Afghan Taliban commrades to fight to the death. At the same time diplomatic efforts to form new administration in Afghanistan were under way. The UN deputy envoy Francesc Vendrel has been holding talks with the Alliance leader and ousted Afghan President Buhanadin Rabani who said he wanted broad-based goverment as soon as possible. He was holding talks also with rival groups within the Northern Alliance whose forces were now in control of large parts of Afghanistan. So the UN is keen to estambish a broad based goverment before the Northern Alliance settled in. The Russians were also sending a delegation to Kabul. The Russian defence minister Sergey Ivanov described the Northern Alliance as the legitimate Goverment of Afghanistan. More than a week after the last independent journalist made contact with Osama ben Laden there was growing speculation as to his whereabouts. A spokesman for the Northern Alliance said Osama ben Laden was still in Afghanistan.

The Americans said they had no reasons to believe he is not in Afghanistan and they were still looking for him. Osama ben Laden was last interviewed by a Pakistani Journalist. Donald Rumsfeld said Osama ben Laden was running out of places to hide in Afghanistan and USA does not believe he was out of the country but it will hunt him down;

The Northern Alliance was reported to negotiate a peaceful surrender of Kunduz but the Taliban said they will surrender only if they were guaranteed a safe passage which was denied by the Northern Alliance. Americans keep asking themselves whether they won the war or not.

19-11-2001

American aircraft have made new attacks on Taliban forces holding out the town of Kunduz-their last stronghold in Northern Afghanistan. B-52 bombers circled above the town and the BBC correspondent saw huge explosions among the Taliban hill-top positions. The Taliban commander in Kunduz Mula Dardula was trying to arrange safe passage for his men out of the town. In Kunduz Taliban were said to kill their commrades who were willing to surrender to the Northern Alliance.

A Family of 7 was killed in American air raids at the town of Gardez South of Kabul. The Family had taken refuge in a distroyed UN building of a mine clearing agency. Gardez had fallen to the Northern Alliance a week ago but the Americans continue to bombard and distroy the town. Foreign envoys were at work in Afghanistan trying to influence the political outcome of the situation there. The UN, Russia, Britain and Iran either sent diplomatic teams to the Capital Kabul. The UN special envoy Francesc Vendrel was hoping to arrange a meeting of Afghan faction leaders within the next few days to discuss the formation of an interim goverment. The UN said it does not want to recognize any particular group or faction as the legitimate goverment of Afghanistan. UN official said that recognition should come as a result of a collective decision of the Afghan people. But since most countries never recognized the Taliban goverment the former President of Afghanistan and Northern Alliance leader Prof. Rabani does still hold Afghan seat at the UN. The UN had said that issue will have to be re-visited at some stage in the future. European Union ministers were meeting in Brussels to review EU foreign and defence policy concentrating on events in Afghanistan and the Middle East. They also assess plans to form a EU rapid reaction force by the year 2oo3. The ministers will be briefed on the continuing visit to the Middle East by an EU delegation which was seeking to boost the peace process. Donald Rumsfeld said the US stepped up its hunt for Osama ben Laden and will not negotiate with Mula Omar the surrender of Kandahar. More special US forces were deployed in Afghanistan and Washington said it will not allow any foreign fighter to slip out in the neighbouring countries. Meanwhile Pakistan closed the Taliban consulate in Pashawa.

20-11-2001

The UN special deputy envoy to Afghanistan Francesc Vendrell completed 4 days of talks with factional leaders. His spokesman said he hopes to make a positive announcement shortly. Vendrell was trying to arrange a conference outside Afghanistan at which the factions would discuss the creation of a broad based goverment. The Northern Alliance which controls the Capital Kabul said the Taliban should not be invited to the conferrence which will take place in Germany on 24 Nov 2oo1. The US said that thousands of Taliban fighters trapped in the town of Kunduz in Northern Afghanistan have only one option:to surrender. The American spokesman in Pakistan Kenton Keat said there were about 12OOO Taliban in Kunduz including some of their best forces along with some 3OOO foreign volunteers;besieged by the Northern Alliance they have been bombed heavily by American aircraft. The Northern Alliance was trying to negotiate an agreement under which the Taliban would surrender their weapons but it said any amnesty would apply only to Afghans not to fereigners;the US goverment said it wants to see the foreign fighters killed or captured. Along with the Taliban there were 3OOOO civilians trapped in Kunduz who were desperate to escape the fighting;as the Americans bombed on the Taliban positions the casualties among the civilians amounted to 5OO a day. Refugees fleeing across the frontline said American raids have hit civilian as well as Taliban targets and there was a growing panic inside the besieged city. Some families said they were forced to flee by the Taliban; other Talibans were selling their guns to pay drivers to take them out of Kunduz.

Western journalist obtained first hand evidence of the extent of the refugee crisis in Southern Afghanistan. A group went in into a Taliban controlled area on the border with Pakistan a saw for a first time a camp occupied by 6Oooo displaced Afghans;all those spoken to said they were forced to leave their homes by American bombing. Many complained of malnutrition and shortages of food and medicine;some said they have not eaten for 1O days. Meanwhile the first consignment of UN aid from Pakistan to Kabul for a week was heading for the Capital in a convoy of nearly 5O trucks. Drivers had until now refused to go in from Pakistan because of the unstable situation.

As the fighting goes on talks on the reconstruction of Afghanistan have begun in Washington;the meeting has been chaired by the US and Japan with 12 other countries attending as well as institutions such as the World Bank, the EU and the Islamic Development Bank. The American Secretary of State Collin Powell said there was a need for reconstruction program which would take many years. Collin Powell also said the US had increased the reward for information leading to the capture of Osama ben Laden: "I have the authority which I will use to authorize an award of up to 25 mio Dollars for the capture of Osama ben Laden". The

Pentagon broadcasted this message several times from a plane flying over Afghanistan and distributed leaflets with that message too.

21-11-2001

Taliban authorities in Afghanistan said they intend to fight on despite losing so much territory to the Northern Alliance. A spokesman of the Taliban leader Mula Omar said they retained control of 4 or 5 provinces. The spokesman Tayab Aga dismissed reports that the Taliban have been negotiating to hand over their main center Kandahar and said they had a duty to defend it: "Tis is a compulsory from our Almighty Allah that we should fight until we are alive to secure our religion and to secure our innocent nation from the looting and robing and killing of the people who want to enter the city". The spokesman repeated that the Taliban were no longer in contact with Osama ben Laden. The General leading the American military campaign in Afghansistan said he was prepaere to use all means of his disposal against the Taliban and Osama ben Laden al Qaida network;General Tomy Francs said that could include the deployment of additional ground troops.

General Franks revealed that he visited Afghanistan on 20 Nov 2001 although nothing was reported to meet leaders of the Northern Alliance;he said he wanted to hear their assessment of the overall situation and discuss coordination between their fighters and US special forces. General Francs said he will stop the bombing of Taliban positions if the Northern Alliance(?) asked him to do so. UN officials said many of their offices in Afghanistan have been looted;an UN spokesman Eric Fout said the UN premises have been ransacked and a convoy with 200 tons of food was high-jacked while under way to the North-Western city of Herat. Tens of thousands of people in Afghanistan are in desperate need of assistance and leading aid agencies have said the lack of security is the main obstacle to delivering food and other supplies.

22-11-2001

Taliban forces encircled in Kunduz-their last stronghold in Northern Afghanistan-were reported to be ready to give up the fight. After intense negotiations the Taliban commander Mula Feysal said his troops would lay down their arms. A spokesman for the Northern Alliance also confirmed that an agreement has been reached but it was unclear whether it covered the tousends of foreigners-mainly Pakistani-fighting with the Taliban in Kunduz. A BBC correspondent in the region said the foreign fighters may choose to fight on because of fear over their faith should they fall in the hands of the Northern Alliance. Reports of a deal have been denied by the Taliban leadership in Kandahar in Southern Afghanistan. Fighting has broken out in the Afghan Capital Kabul where the Northern Alliance was trying to dislodge pocket of a Taliban forces;700 Taliban fighters and 400 foreigners were holding out in ridge overlooking a village Midensharh 30 km South-West of Kabul. Other reports said the Taliban were 2000 dug in into mountain positions. The attack started after peace talks collapsed. The local Taliban

Commander Gula Mohamed is said to have accepted money to defect but than stayed in the hills apparently fearing reprisals because of his reputation of brutality when he controlled the area. The Northern Alliance troops were backed by tanks but latest reports said they met stiffer resistance than expected and retreated. The Northern Alliance had sked the US in vain for air support to bombard the Taliban positions.

The British foreign Secretary Jack Straw was in Iran for talks about the future of Afghanistan; Iran called against foreign troops in Afghanistan which would complicate the situation. Jack Straw said British troops won't remain longer than necessary. He had also talks with the foreign affairs spokesman for the Northern Alliance Abdulah Abdulah. A BBC correspondent in Teheran said Jack Straw called the meeting very constructive and reassuring. Abdulah Abdulah said they talked at length about the need of broad based goverment to which he said the Northern Alliance was fully comitted. Asked if that would include moderate elements of the Taliban Abdulah Abdulah replied that there was a contradiction in terms. Jack Straw was to have talks with senior leaders in Iran later and than goes on to Pakistan ahead an UN conference on the future of Afghanistan which begins in Bonn-Koenigswinter on 26 Nov 2o01.

Pakistan said it ordered the closure of the Taliban Embassy in Islamabad; a foreign ministry's spokesman said the decision was taken yesterday and communicated to the Taliban today. Staff was given a reasonable time to wind up their affairs. A BBC correspondent in Islamabad said the move brings to an end the close relationship between Pakistan and the former Afghan rulers. The Pakistanis have already announced the end of the diplomatic ties and a spokesman said they allowed the Embassy to remain open as the only official channel for communicating with the Taliban. The closure came after the US said it saw no reason for the office to remain open and disclosed that it will be discussing the matter with the Pakistani authorities. The Taliban Ambassador expressed disappointment at the decision of the authorities to close the last Taliban diplomatic outpost. The Ambassador Abdul Salam Zaif said the move would complicate humanitarian relief efforts in Afghanistan by making contacts with world organizations involved more difficult but he said the move was no surprise-the closure followed pressure from the US.

The Embassy had provided an international plattform for the Taliban to give their version of the fighting and arial bombing of Afghnaistan.

After fall of darkness the Northern Alliance began the long waited assault on Kunduz where thousands of Taliban remained surrounded by the forces of the Northern Alliance;the attack started despite frantic last minute efforts to negotiate a surrender and conflicting reports said Taliban leaders inside the city had agrreed to lay down their weapons. Taliban troops responded with mortar rounds. But the returning fire was soon drawned out by the thunder of bombs raining down on Taliban positions from American bombers high above. Even as the advance began Northern commander continued to insist that a surrender is stil possible. But with tanks and troops pushing their way down the road to Kunduz it appears that time for a talking has come to an end. Local UN officials in Afghanistan have asked the Americans to stop dropping food packets in certain areas. A person was blown his head and others maimed after mistaking unexploded yellow cluster bomb for the food packets which are the same bright yellow color.

23-11-2001

The Pakistani foreign minister Abdul Satar has called for special efforts by the international community to end the fighting in Afghanistan and promote reconsiliation. He was speaking after a meeting in Islamabad with the British foreign minister Jack Straw. He said a humanitarian disater was possible in the besieged city of Kunduz. Jack Straw said that the Northern Alliance should accept the surrender of those Taliban fighters who wanted to give themselves up but for those who had been fighting for the Taliban could not expect to get free. Jack Straw also met the Pakistani President General Pervaze Musharaf and both expressed their support for the rapid establishment of a broad based goverment in Afghanistan. Northern Alliance forces in Afghanistan said they gained some ground in the battle for Kunduz where thousands of Taliban fighters were surrounded. Alliance commanders said they have driven the Taliban out of hilltop positions around Kunduz and 100 more Taliban soldiers have give themselves up. But Taliban resistance was continuing and American B-52 bombers have been back in action in the besieged city. The continuing fighting came as some Northern Alliance commanders said they're still trying to negotiate a Taliban surrender. Kunduz occupies a strategic position controlling links to neighbouring Tajikistan. There were fears of heavy casualties of the Taliban and their foreign allies fight to the finish in the city. Northern Alliance forces have also renewed their assault on Taliban fighters dug in along the hills round Midensharh 30 km South from Kabul. The fighters have stayed there following the general withdrawal from Kabul by the Taliban 2 weeks earlier. Alliance forces first launched their attack on 22 Nov but were beaten back. A BBC correspondent said there were some 1000 Taliban dug in round Midensharh but it was not clear whether they were surrounded by Alliance forces. One Alliance commander told the BBC that the Taliban had a supply route open to the South which they can use as a mean of escape.

24-11-2001

There were growing indications that the siege of Kunduz-the Taliban last remaining stronghold in Northern Afghanistan was coming to an end;to the applause of the besieging Northern Alliance troops jeeps and tanks driven by Taliban soldiers crossed the frontline East of the city. Northern Alliance forces surrounding Kunduz were predicting a general surrender of the city within 24 hours. BBC correspondent Ruppert Winfield Haze reported from just outside Kunduz, that after days of speculations and rumours the surrender of Taliban troops inside Kunduz has finally began. On the front 20 km East of the city a column of 20 Taliban vehicles streamed across the lines;Northern Alliance troops waved and clapped as the Taliban vehicles beat their horns and flashed their lights. It was less a surrender than a wholesale defection. Northern Alliance commanders around 1000 Taliban surrendered. On the other side of Kunduz Alliance commander general Abdul Rashid Dostum said another 600 Taliban surrendered to his forces including some foreign fighters. A confrontation between Taliban troops and Northern Alliance forces around Midensharh South-West of Kabul had ended peacefully with an estimated 2000 Taliban handing over their heavy weapons to the Alliance. A Taliban commander told the BBC his fighters would be allowed to go home. Meanwhile clashes have been reported between Taliban forces and Pashtoon tribal fighters on the essential supply route between the Taliban stronghold Kandahar and the Pakistani border. The Taliban denied that they have lost any territory. Eyewitnesses said 8 people were killed in an airstrike in a village close to the border.

The Green Party in Gemany was debating the goverment decision to offer military support to the US war in Afghanistan. Senior Party members warned that failures to back Chansellor Schroeder's offer will certainly lead to a govement's collapse. But the Green Party co-leader Claudia Roth was told the BBC she was unsure how delegates would vote.

British foreign office minister Ben Bradshow was sprinkled with blood by anti-war protester.

Food convoy with 40 tons of food reached the Capital Kabul and was distributed there among the population. A Swuiss-Air plane crashed near Zurich;the reasons for the crash are still unknown.

25-11-2001

The siege of the Taliban-held city of Kunduz in Northern Afghanistan appears to be in its final stage. Today 100 more Taliban soldiers defected crossing the lines into Northern Alliance territory. The Alliance forces were moving towards the city. It took shorter than many expected but the collapse of the Taliban control in the city of Kunduz appears now a virtual certainity. Late this afternoon a long column of Northern Alliance tanks and armoured personnel carriers began rolling towards the city. News came from further up the road that the small town of Hanabad 20 km North of Kunduz had fallen without a shot. Hours earlier hundreds of Taliban defectors had poured across the frontlines in jeeps and pickups surrendering themselves to the Northern Alliance. Reports from the North of the city said a thousand more Taliban gave themselves up there. Northern Alliance commander said they are prepared to enter the city on Monday morning-26-11-2oo1.

The Northern Alliance leader and former Afghan President Buhanadin Rabani said fears that captured foreign fighters will be masacred were baseless. The statement follows concern from the Western coalition of a possible bloodbath in Kunduz. He said he had ordered his commanders around Kunduz not to harm any foreigners who surrendered or were captured, reported the BBC.

correspondent in Kabul Peter Grester. "It is a great lie we want to kill them", he told a news conference in the Presidential Palace in Kabul, "we will investigate them and than hand them to the UN for repatriation". This statement was not true because there were no UN troops in Afghanistan. This repatriatiation even despite an incident in which some Arab prisoners reportedly blew themselves and one senior Alliance commander up with a hidden grenade: "The Northern Alliance would disarm and send Afghan Taliban fighters to their homes", said Buhanadin Rabani further. However reports from Mazar-e Sharif said that revolts of captured Taliban prisoners and foreign Arab fighters had continued all night long at the the Kala-Jungi prison complex and American planes and special forces were called in to suppress them.

Mazar-e Sharif was under the control of the Northern Alliance General Abdul Rashid Dostum.2 senior Alliance commanders were killed and another injured after the Taliban broke into amunition depot and weaponed themselves;heavy fighting with the Northern Alliance ensued for several hours. A spokesman said there were large numbers of deads on both sides. The Pentagon confirmed its war planes bombed parts of the complex Kala-Jungi in which the Taliban prisoners were kept in support of the National Alliance forces. A BBC correspondent in Mazar-e Sharif said the revolt began after one prisoner threw a hand grenade killing his guards. Other reports said that all 800 prisoners at Kala-Jungi prison near Mazar-e Sharif were killed and no captives taken. At Kunduz itself Northern Alliance commanders said they were preparing to take control of the city after the surrender of hundreds of Taliban fighters. Aid agencies will follow them in the city where were several thousands civilian casualties after 10 days of US air strikes. Early reports said that Kunduz was taken by the Commander Daud but this was later contradicted;commander Daud took the town of Hanabad. Kandahar is still under Taliban control, reported BBC correspondent Daniel Lakh in Quetta. "The Western media does not cover this war sufficiently", said Guram Farukhazam-former minister of Buhanadin Rabani, now living in exile in London and chairman of the Afghan Forum in London.

26-11-2001

1500 American Marines have taken control of an air base 100 km South-West from Kandahar-the main Taliban stronghold As helicopters rolled in with men and equipment residents of Kandahar heard loud explosions. Additional marines are expected to be sent in over the coming days to support anti-Taliban forces. BBC correspondent reported from the Pakistani city of Quetta, that this deployment came rapidly over night;waves of American helicopters carrying armoured vehicles in slings ferried in 1500 US marines. There was fearce American bombardment of Kandahar beforehand and later reports spoke of renewed air attacks. However it is difficult to confirm any information coming out from Southern Afghanistan at the moment. But the marines have certainly established the most signifficant beach-head of this conflict 7 weeks after the war began and seems to be almost over. US officials said the deployment of US forces would continue in the next few days with additional 1500 men eventually on the ground in South Afghanistan.

Pres. Bush said the troops were part of the operation to hunt down those linked to the September attacks on the US. In Pentagon briefing the defence secretary Donald Rumsfeld said this hunt would not end in Afghanistan: "Our job does not end in Afghanistan and with the Taliban and with al Qaida or even with Osama ben Laden ;Afghanistan is only the begining of our efforts in the world. We are comitted to a war on terrorism and this war will not end until terrorists with global reach will be found and stopped and defeated". The US troops distroyed column of 15 Taliban vehicles near the air prot where they landed. President Bush said the risc of American casualties has risen but he did not believe they will capture Mula Mohamed Omar: "He is not the kind that will surrender!", he said. The next target will be Saddam Husein, if he does not let in US weapon inspectors, President Bush announced. Asked by journalists what will happen if he does not, he answered: " Saddam Husein will find out".

Fighting was still going on in fort Kala-Jungi near Mazar-e Sharif where hundreds of Taliban prisoners staged a revolt against their captors. A leading figure in the Northern Alliance in Mazar-e Sharif Dr. Abdul Rahid told the BBC that Taliban prisoners were still holding out in the Southern wing of the fort. He said the revolt began when the prisoners who still were carrying hand grenades started killing their guards indiscriminately. The city of Kunduz-the Taliban's last stronghold in Northern Afghanistan-has finally fallen to the Northern Alliance. BBC reporter Ruppert Winfield Haze arrived in the city and reported from there, in the main basar huge crowds of currious people, soldiers, tanks and armoured personal carriers. Local people said the Taliban left late last night so that the Northern Alliance could enter the city in the morning unopposed. Another journalist however said that the forces of general Daud met fierce resistence. A large group of foreign Taliban retreated to the South of the city near the city's air port and were airlifted by a large number of Pakistani aircraft coming into the airport over night which were believed evacuating the foreign Taliban to Pakistan. It was impossible to confirm this reports but the situation in the center of Kunduz was sofar calm and the Northern Alliance was reported to be in complete control. Later reports however said that wounded Taliban soldiers were beaten, kicked, punched, lashed and executed in the streets. Many of them were also dragged on the backs of trucks. Flyes were buzzing over their lifeless bodies. General Abdul Rashid Dustam told the BBC that 6OOO Taliban fighters were captured. He again offered assurances that prisoners' rights would be respected and said it was up to the UN to decide what to do with them. He did n o t say what would happen to those Taliban soldiers who did not surrender. An US bomb fell astray the fort of Kala-Jungi killing 6 Northern Alliance soldiers and 5 Americans. The Pentagon said the bomb was dropped to try to suppress a revolt by hundreds of captured Taliban soldiers. The US soldiers were trying to guide the bombers to the part of the fort still controlled by the Taliban. A BBC correspondent said at 2O:oo GMT that the fighting was still going on and there have been hundreds of casualties among the Taliban prisoners and the Northern Alliance. SUmmary executions also took place. In Kandahar anti-Taliban Pashtoon tribes captured the main road between Kandahar and Spin-Boldak close to the Pakistani border. 14 men were arrested in Belgium on suspicion for the aassessination of Northen Alliance Commander Ahmed Sha Massud on o9 Sept 2oo1. The prosecution said the killers travelled on stolen Belgian passports. The EU Arab league demanded the dismissal of the Belgian Justice minister Verwighen because he issued a racist report.

27-11-2001

Egyptian foreign minister Ahmed Aha visited the US for talks with the US foreign minister Collin Powell.

The riots in Kala-Jungi-prison complex near Mazar-e Sharif still continued;special US and British troops were called in to suppress the rebelion. US air craft were bombing the prison complex all night long. Meanwhile Russian troops arrived in Kabul. They said their mission was to establish a mobile field hospital. Their arrival wakened sensitive feelings;12 Russian airplanes with equipment arrived at the Bagram airport near Kabul. The Russians held Afghanistan under occupation till 1989.

Rival tribal leaders arrived in Germany for talks. The meeting was held in Koenigsberg near Bonn. The German foreign minister Joshka Fisher addressed the participants in broken English. He spoke at length about the German role in Afghanistan and the way the Germans are going to help Afghans. The conference was covered by the BBC Newshour journalist Alex Prody and the BBC Pashtoon service journalist Baka Moin among others. The landmark conference will discuss the shape of an interim goverment for Afghanistan. In an address the UN Special Envoy to Afghanistan Lacta Brahimi read out a message from the UN secretary general Kofi Anan urging the Afghan delegates not to repeat the mistakes of the past. He told them to prove the sceptics wrong and choose the path of compromise over conflict.

The representative of the Northern Alliance Yunice Khanuni made also a very eloquent speech about the mistakes of the past and the way they want to keep Afghanistan united and to move towards democracy and human rights. The King's representative talks about Islam and democracy. Altogether the delegates were very optimistic that this conference will bring about a transitional period for Afghanistan in which reconstruction and proper goverment and Constitution will be the start. All sides agreed over the creation of a broad based goverment after the collapse of the Taliban.

The former governer of the Western Afghan city of Herat Ismail Khan has issued an appeal for urgent international help "to stay off eminent humanitarian disaster". Ismail Khan told the BBC that some 100000 refugees from the highlands of the Khor and Badris provinces North and East were heading for Herat in hope of survival. An estimated 100000 people were on the road trying desperately to get to Herat. The city and the nearby refugee camps have been already swamped by hundreds of new arrivals every day. The camps were full there were no facilities for the newcomers. Ismail Khan said that if an immediate international relief operation was not forthcoming a humanitarian disaster would be inevitable. "People are already dying" he said. A Swedish TV cameraman covering the conflict in Afghanistan was killed by gunmen;Wulf Strongberg was shot shot by a group of armed robbers who broke into the house where he was staying with other Swedish journalists in the Northern town of Talokan. The Canadian journalist Malcolm Hix was kidnapped and held for ransom near the South Afghan town of Spin Boldak.

The mutiny of the Taliban prisoners in the Kala-Jungi prison complex near Mazar-e Sharif ended in a bloodbath after the last Taliban fighters were killed by a tank fire. British and

American special troops were also called in to suppress the mutiny. The Guardian-journalist Luc Harding saw the Taliban surrounded by hundreds of lifeless corpses of their comrades, said he in a phone interview for the BBC. Amnesty International said it will launch an investigation into the blood bath of Kala-Jungi prison complex; only yesterday General Abdul Rashid Dustam vowed the prisoners would be handed to the UN, although there were no UN troops in Afghanistan. The US continued re-inforcing their troops at a military base 100 km South-West from the Taliban stronghold of Kandahar. Additional 600 US marines arrived their "to hunt down terrorists", as Donald Rumsfeld put it. The US started a formal procedure to get the Algerian born pilot Lofti Raici extradited from the UK;the british authorities accused him of falisfying a pilot's application while the Americans consider him directly involved in the September attacks.

27-11-2001

Afghan delegates attending a conference in the German city of Bonn-Konigswinter said they all accept the principle of broad based goverment in their country following the collapse of the Taliban regime there. The UN spokesman of the conference said that it was encouraging to hear that they were all speaking with one voice. The BBC diplomatic correspondent reported from the conference, the UN spokesman Ahmed Fousi said the Afghan parties had set themselves the aim of reaching an agreement within 3-5 days. The agenda they have adopted covered the arrengements for a transition to a new broad based goverment together with measures to ensure security of the people of Afghanistan. The UN would like the conference to approve the establishment of 2 bodies that would run the country withnin the next 2 months:the small interim administration or cabinett and a large interim council or parliament. Ahmed Fousi said that at the end of this period a traditional assembly in Afghanistan-a loya jirgha-would approve an administration and a council to hold office to up to 2 years. The UN called this longer lived bodies "transitional". Afghan delegates at a conference in Germany on the political future of their country were expected to get down to hard bargaining today on the startegy for putting a goverment in place in Kabul. Delegates representing the Northern Alliance and only 3 other factions were meeting the UN official in charge of the talks Lakhta Brahimi. A BBC correspondent at the conference said the Allince which was aleady in Kabul and one other delegetaion are less in a hurry to install a goverment there than the other 2.

The UN deputy envoy to Afghanistan Francesk Vendrell warned that full agreement may not be reachead on the future of Afghanistan. He said the atmosphere at the conference was positive but difficult negotiatians lie ahead especially on whether the UN must send in multinational UN peace keeping force. He said the 4 delegations were still holding separate meetings to get to know each other;all the parties had to accept that when elections get under way in 3-years time there would be winners as well as losers, he added.

A mutiny of Taliban prisoners in fort Kala-Jungi near Mazar-e Sharif ended after a 3 days of battle described as the bloodiest yet in the Afghan war;a sery of detonating explosions was heard when the revolt was finally quelled aa the last 2 prisoners still holding out were killed by a tank fire. Red Crosse officials and journalist were allowed in fort Kal-Jungi near Mazar-e Sharif to see the carnege left there after a 3 day revolt by Taliban prisoners. A BBC journalist-one of the first to went in the compound saw hundreds of dead bodies thrown around. Thousands of pieces of grenades and bombs covered the ground. The Red Cross was assessing how many Taliban were killed as Northern Alliance forces backed by American airpower and special US ground forces tried to put down the uprising. The human rights organisation Amnesty International called for an inquiry into the deaths. General Abdul Rashid Dustam who was in the charge of fort Kal-Jungi denied the prisoners were ill-treated. He said the blood bath began when one of them blew up a grenade at a general who'd been sent to assure that the prisoners were well looked after. The British goverment denied any responsibility for the massacre in Kala-Jungi but a senior Labour MP said an inquiry was nessecary. One CIA-agent died in the battle of Kala-Jungi;it is not clearwhat role played the American special forces there.

The Americans said their planes bombed a compound used by the Taliban leadership and al Qaida network during action in Kandahar area yesterday. The Taliban last Ambassador to Pakistan Abdul Zaif said the Taliban leader Mula Omar was still safe. He said the attack were to the North and East of Kandahar an hit a Taliban convoy rather than a training camp. Abdul Zaif said the situation inside Kandahar was now normal although the city's airport was under heavy bombardment by the Americans. US helicopters and transport planes have been flying more men and equipment into the airstrip base established outside Kandahar at 25 Nov 2oo1 just 1OO km South West from Kandahar. Truck drivers between Herat and Kandahar refused to drive food supplies after American planes hit an distroyed by rocket fire 4o trucks loaded with food and blankets; the supply was import from Iran into Afghanistan. Germany and France warned the US not to extended its campaign to other countries such as Somalia, Iraq or Sudan. German Chansellor Gerhard Schroeder warned that Germany will not join any action in these countries;the French defence minister Alan Richard said there was no evidence these countries were involved in terrorism.

29-11-2oo1

Afghan delegates to the conference in Germany on the future of their country have expressed optimism about the prospects of reaching agreement. One report quotes a Northern Alliance official said a deal was reached in principle with the team representing the ex-King Zahir Shah on the shape of an interim administration.

However the BBC correspondent on the talks said the difficulty would come with the fine details. It was not clear if the delegations will be able to agree on who should be represented on the body and who should lead it. UN official said the quicker the parties can make progress the more it will encourage the international community to start putting in massive funds for promised reconstruction.

The Taliban leader Mula Omar called on his fighters to continue resisting the American forces in Afghanistan. In an address to his men over military radios Mula Omar said there was no need for negotiations and no question of surrender. The Taliban were reported to be still firmly in control of their Southern stronghold Kandahar despite the increasing military pressure in the area. There was some overnight bombing in and around the city but no word of the targets were: were they civil targets?Additional US marines were sent to the airstrip they were holding 120 South-West from Kandahar raising the number there from 600 to 800. The Amiricans said they will now concentrate on try to break the coordination of the Taliban and al Qaida network by cutting off the leaders from their troops.

The Taliban have hanged publically a man accused of spying for the Americans;he was directing the American bombers by a satelite telephone.

30-11-2001

George Harrison died in Los Angelos aged 58.

As delegations from 4 Afghan factions met a senior UN official at the start of a key conference to determin the country's political future the British foreign secretary Jack Straw said there was more progress than anticipated at the meeting.

The Northern Alliance who lead the military campaign against the Talibans said all delegation at the Bonn conference now agreed that the country's former King Zahir Shah should play a leading role in any future interim administration. An Alliance spokesman also confirmed that they were prepared to accept the UN peace keeping force. However one delegate walked out of the conference:Hadgi Abdul Kadir said the Pashtoons were underrepresented.

The 4 delegations were yet trying to reach an agreement on the specific details of an interim administrtion for the country. A BBC correspondent at the conference said that the delegations have still to agree on the compositions of the interim bodies who will run the country. The legitimacy of the Bonn talks was questioned by the former Afghan President Buhanadin Rabani;he argued that only the principal should be agreed in Bonn and that the final details should be debated in Kabul.

In Afghanistan itself American war planes have been bombing Taliban sheltering in bunkers at the airport of Kandahar-the last city held by Taliban troops. BBC correspondent Suzanne Price sent this report from the border city of Quetta in Pakistan: "A spokesman for anti-Taliban fighters backing the former governer of Kandahar said they were about 6 km from Kandahar airport. He said American planes were bombing the airport but there was no fighting on the ground. The anti-Taliban forces in the South a group to various Mujaheddin commanders and clan leaders have yet to form an united coalition. The all come from the largest ethnic group-the Pashtoons-and none of them wants to see the Northern Alliance who come from differnt ethnic backgrounds expanding into that area". A tribal commander outside Kandahar said today's raids were among the fiercest since the start of the war. He said US planes were targetting a large number os suspected Taliban and al Qaida sites in and around Kandahar including 2 garrissons and weapon depots to the West! Several thousands Pashtoon fighters opposed to the Taliban are ammased close to the airport South of Kandahar but said they have no immediate plans to advance. More than 1000 US marines have been now flown into the desert airfield outside of Kandahar which was seized from the Taliban on 25 Nov. A spokesman for the Americans confirmed that a suspected leader of Osama bin Laden's Al Qaida network has been captured in Afghanistan by the Northern Alliance forces and will be handed over to the Americans shortly. Ahmed Abdul Rahman is the son of the blinded Eqyptian cleric Omar Abdul Rahman currently in jail in the US for his role in the bombing of the World Trade Center in 1993. The American spokesman Kenton Keat said Ahmed Abdul Rahman had close links with al Qaida;American media reports said he was involved in training recruits to the al Qaida network. Tribal Pashtoon leaders were surrounding Kandahar before they make their final push on the city.

The foreign ministers of Pakistan and Iran gathered to discuss the situation in Afghanistan after the removal of the Taliban;they said relations between the two countries will improve by the overthrow of the Taliban regime in Afghanistan. The Pakistani foreign minister Abdul Satar said that a shadow that had clouded ties between Islamabad and Teheran had disappeared. His Iranian counterpart Kamal Kharazy said both countries could now play an important role in an establishment of a new goverment in Afghanistan and in the reconstruction of the country. The BBC islamic affairs analyst said relations between Shiaat Muslim Iran and mainly Suni Muslim Pakistan have long been tainted with suspicion as they fight for influence in Afghanistan.

Iraq recalled his Ambassador to Turkey because of alleged contacts to al Qaida network.

01-10-2001

Talks on the future of Afghanistan have gone into their 5th day but the problem of sharing out power among the various factions of the country is still unresolved. The delegations have agreed in principle on political structures for an interim administration, a parliamentary stile supreme council and a cabinett but hte delegates meeting in Koenigswinter still could not agree who gets which portfolios. Delegates at the conference said the emphasis now had switched to the composition of a small interim executive. Discussions on a larger parliament have been put aside among with disagreements within the Northern Alliance. BBC correspondent Barnaby Mason reported from Bonn: "It is hard to say whether the change of direction in the negotiations is a good or a bad sign for the outcome of the conference. The UN was still hoping for a deal on powersharing sometime today its original target. But the talks have been bobbed down in the problem of getting agreement on the composition of a large interim council of some 200 members. Thinges were made worse by blocking tactics of the older Northern Alliance leaders in Kabul to the evident exasperation of the head of the Alliance delegation Yonuz Khanuni. In a reference to these divisions British goverment officials have critisized saying Britain would give no support to anyone seeking to hold up the process. Progress have been held up by the failure of the Northern Alliance to provide its list of name for 2 proposed interim bodies: a small executive and the much larger supreme council. They would run Afghanistan for the next few months;the list was apparently blocked by elements of the Northern Alliance leadership in Kabul in particular by Burhanudin Rabani-the president in the old Alliance goverment. Now Reuters was quoting the leader of the delegation there Yonuz Khanuni has saying he would seek popular support to strike a deal if Mr. Rabani continued to block the list".

A week after revolt of Taliban prisoners at fort Kala-Jungi near the Afghan city of Mazar-e Sharif a number of survivors have been found alive in the basement of the complex. A photo journalist from the New York Times James Hill told the BBC that many of the prisoners were seriously wounded with bullet wounds to the legs or to the chests. "Several of the Taliban prisoners need operations, mainly they have lost limbs from bullets or hit by shrapnels;I spoke to Red Cross officials and they said several of them need operation many have lost limbs hit by bullets or shrapnels. Nearly all of them are in very serious state. I would say that probably a third of them are seriously wounded" James Hill said that most of the prisoners were mostly non-Afghan Taliban fighters. Their faces were chared and blackened after Northern Alliance forces poured oil into the basement and set it alight. Yesterday the UN Human Rights commissioner Marry Robinson backed calls for an inquiry into the mass assessination. Hundreds of Taliban prisoners died in the riot as Northern Alliance backed by American special forces fought to regain control of fort Kala-Jungi. 9O Taliban fighters surrendered today after the Northern Alliance flooded the basement of Kala-Jungi with water to expell the non-Afghan Taliban fighters. Nearly a third of them need medical treatment for injuries and wounds inflicted by the Northern Alliance troops.

02-12-2001

Amerian warplanes continued airstrikes on the remaining Taliban position in their stronghold Kandahar;forces opposed to the Taliban say they were continuing to advance towards the city. The Pashtoon militia said they were just outside the airport and they have clashed with Taliban fighters. BBC correspondent Suzanne Price reported from Kandahar(?):

"The area around the last Taliban stronghold Kandahar was once again subjected to heavy bombardment by American warplanes. But there was still no sign that the Taliban were willing to surrender. There have been various reports of civilian casualties. One man who arrived in the Pakistani border town of Chaman said American bombs hit his village between the city and the airport killing 15 residents including 5 of his children. More than 1OOO American marines were stationed at the air strip South-West of Kandahar. They have been carrying out patrols but have not been sofar involved in any fighting. Donals Rumsfeld said that all Taliban who do not surrender will be killled".

The UN said it hopes to finalize an agreement on Monday between the Afghan factions who negotiate the country's political future. A UN spokesman at the conference in Germany told correspondents a draft plan presented to the factions was affirmed by the interim authority of some 3O representatives to run Afghanistan for 6 months. The spokesman said all that was missing was the agreement of the main factions to a list of names of who should serve on this interim executive.

03-12-2001

Anti-Taliban forces took parts of the Hatkliz-province in which is Kandahar. They took also parts of Kandahar airport. Anti-Taliban commander Mohamed Zeman said 100 civilians were killed in the past 3 days after US planes hit the wrong targets near Tula-Bura.

Delegations from Afghanistans 4 main factions were preparing to meet the UN special representative Lakhta Brahimi to discuss the draft document on the political future of Afghanistan. A BBC correspondent at the conference near the German city of Bonn said now follows the most difficult part of the talks-the allocation of posts in the cabinett which would govern Afghanistan for the next 6 months.2 possible candidates to head the body are the leader of the former Afghan King's delegation Professor Abdul Zatar Zirat and an influential Pashtoon tribal leader Hamed Kharzy, whose forces are fighting the Taliban. Conference sources said the increasing weary delegates and officials were now in the last stages of negotiations. Forces loyal to Hamed Kharzy said they have taken the district of Hahriz from the Taliban as they advanced from the North on Kandahar. Other anti-Taliban forces said they have now captured part of Kandahar air port and were engaged in a fierce battle for the main terminal building. US planes have continued heavy bombing close to Kandahar but Taliban official said their defences have not been severely damaged. American planes also conducted raids on the mountain range South of Jalalabad where Osama ben Laden was reported to have sought refuge.

04-12-2001

Taliban forces round Kandahar formed a body trying to persuade Mula Omar to surrender Kandahar. Talks on the future of Afghanistan resumed today in Bonn after a session produced agreement late on Monday on the formation of an interim goverment for the next 6 months. Today's remaining task is denominating members of the participating factions to specific goverment posts with a view of overall accord on Wendesday. The top job of the interim administration may go the Pashtoon leader Hamed Kharzy who was currently fighting the Taliban near their stronghold in Kandahar. The draft document reached on Mondday includes provisions on the deployment of international security force in the Capital Kabul and a symbolic role for the exiled King Zahir Shah. 150 names were submitted for 29 posts. The UN began an emergency food distribution scheme for 1000000 people in the Afghan Capital Kabul. The UN World Food Programe said it employed over 3000 men and women to help carry out the distribution; they will be visiting the poorest areas of the city to determine how many people are in each household and to assess their needs. They were also distributing food coupons.

British journalist Richard Loyd Pari said there were 120 killed civilians and anti-Taliban fighters in villages South of Jalalabad where American planes missed their targets. The journalist said there was no indications that Taliban or al Qaida members were in the area and the killed were civilians rather than Taliban. Donald Rumsfeld said already this were manipulated rumours. Anti-Taliban fighters retreated from the Kandahar airport after they met fierce resistence from Arab fighters.

05-12-2001

Among the prisoners in Kala-Jungi prison complex was discovered John Walker-young American who fought for the Taliban in Mazar-e Sharif. His Father was Irish catholic, his Mother buddhist. He converted to Islam when he was 16. Donald Rumsfeld said he will be trialed by a secrete anti-terror military court. An American aircraft has accidentally bombed US-special forces killing 3 American soldiers and wounding 19 others. A number of Afghan anti-Taliban fighters working together with the US soldiers were also killed or injured. The Defence Department in Washington said it was investigating the cause of the incident which happened North of the city of Kandahar. It said the attack involved a guided bomb equipped for a special navigation system but it was not clear why it fell in the wrong place. Hamed Kharzy was also hurt in the raid after a B-52 missed its target.

5 Americans were hurt when a similar weapon went astray in November in Northern Afghanistan;this is the first time we learnt for the accident. The Pentagon said it was not clear if it was an equipment failure or the bomb went astary. The French Agency Medicines sans frontier said in the past 4 days 80 civilians were killed in American raids near Tura Bura mountain base;the Agency transported 50 other wounded bodies. The Pentagon denied this report saying that ALL BOMBS hit their targets. Reports from Eastern Afghanistan said anti-Taliban forces including American special forces had launched an attack on Tura Bura mountain base where is believed Osama ben Laden may be hiding. Tanks fired repeated volleys into the mountain side complex. The anti-Taliban fighters were supported by American planes which were bombing the base for days;this was reported only now. Elsewhere Taliban fighters resisted an offensive on the airport at Kandahar-their last stronghold.

After 8 days of intense negotiations an agreement was finally signed in Koenigswinter on the transitional goverment to run Afghanistan following the collaps of the Taliban. The delegates agreed that the Pashtoon tribal commander Hamed Kharzy would head the 29-members administration. Yonuz Khanuni was elected for interim interior minister;the Northern Alliance got 17 seats. The new goverment will take power on 22 December 2001. The UN special envoy to Afghanistan Lakhta Brahimi said delgates must leave up to their commitments to reconciliation, human rights and the rule of law. BBC diplomatic correspondent reported from the conference, "Yonuz Khanuni said the result had proved, the Afghans had proved they can not only fight they can make also and compromise. Hedayat Amin Afsala became the new finance minister; he is from the group centered around the former King of Afghanistan Zahir Shah. He said it will be a tough job but he was looking forward to it. From the German Chancellor Gerhardt Schroeder there was pure delight;he said that time takes some credit for the successful outcome and he stressed that it have shown the role the UN should and could play in resolving this these kind of conflicts". Hamed Kharzy said his main priorities will be peace and stability. He told the BBC he tought that Taliban would hand over power to local tribal chiefs and clergy in those provinces still under Taliban control. He also said he could forsee a role for a UN-led peace keeping force. Under the agreement the Northern Alliance will hold the defence, interior and foreign ministries with ministers Rabani, Khanuni and Abdula. Many will see the interim body as a puppet administration working for the Americans.

06-12-2001

09:00 GMT

The man named as Afghanistan's new leader Hamed Khrazy is due to make an announcement on the faith of Kandahar-the last city held by the Taliban in the South of the country. A Taliban spokesman was quated to say the Taliban leader Mula Omar has agreed to surrender Kandahar but there was no confirmation. Hamed Kharzy who was in Southern Afghanistan for a number of weeks to negotiated with tribesmen said that he would offer an amnesty for Taliban fighters but not for Mula Omar himself and he will not be awarded the medal of freedom, as Donald Rumsfeld put it. Hamed Kharzy was as a leader chosen for Afghanistan's new interim goverment which is due to take power in Kabul later in December.

17:00 GMT

A deal was made for the surrender of Kandahar. Speaking from Kandahar a Taliban spokesman told the BBC Taliban would surrender the city to oppposition forces led by the man named as Afghanistan's new leader Hamed Kharzy. Hamed Kharzy said that the surrender would be unconditional. He said he had assured the Taliban of their safety if they lay down their arms. But he refused to be drawn on the faith of the Taliban leader Mula Omar saying that he would be treated as other Afghans. Some reports have suggested that the handover could take place on Friday; Hamed Kharzy said the practicality of the Taliban surrender were still worked out. The American Defence Secretary Donald Rumsfeld said that the US would not be in favour of any deal with the Taliban that would allow their leader Mula Omar to remain free and live in dignity;he said he did not want Mula Omar be awarded the medall of freedom as he put it. Donald Rumsfeld said the US wanted justice but there were different ways it could be achieved. The British Prime Minister Tony Blair said the Taliban's agreement to surrender Kandahar was a total vindication of the strategy worked out from the start by the Western Alliance. Other reports said however that Kandahar will be surrendered to Pashtoon tribal leader Mula Nagibulla and the Taliban will retain their weapons. There will be amnesty also for Mula Omar if he denounce terrorism and disossiates from his friends. However Americans prefer to see him dead rather than put on trial. At 23:30 GMT a report came in that the Taliban lost the airport of Kandahar;it did not say to which forces.

Reports from Afghanistan suggest there is split in the Northern Alliance following the multiparty agreement on a new interim administration. One of the Alliance's leading military commanders Abdul Rashid Dustam had said he will not take part in the new goverment. His complaint in a BBC interview was that he was promised control over the foreign ministry as award for his army efforts'in capturing Mazar-e Sharif from the Taliaban. "That was the begin of the downfall of the Taliban", he said. General Dustam is not the only Alliance member said to be unhappy with the Bonn agreement. Other factions complained that Jamiat Islami-the largest party with Indian lines-has the bulk of the top jobs including the 3 power ministries. There are further signs of disaffection within the Northern Alliance over the multi-party agreement on a new interim Afghan administration. The former governer of the Western city of Herat Ismail Khan who controls most of Western Afghanistan accused delegates at the conference in Bonn of negotiating positions for themselves. He said the allocation of posts within the new goverment failed to take into account realities on the ground. Another prominent Alliance commander-Abdul Rashid Dustam-has also angrily denounced the Agreement and threatened to boykott the new goverment;he commands a large military force in the North of Afghanistan.

Officials of the UNHCR have expressed concern over reports that Pakistan is planing to move Afghan refugees out of urban areas into refugee camps-a move widely seen as a first step towards repatriating them. The UNHCR said it opposes any plan which involves forcibly picking out refugees from existing communities and moving them against their will. A BBC correspondent in Pakistan said the plan could be an attempt to apiese growing public impatience there as many Pakistanis see the refugees as a growing financial burden at time of economic hardship.

A court in London has found 9 Afghan men guilty of high-jacking a plane from Kabul to Briatain. They were part of a group that took over in Afghan Airlines plane in February 2000 and forced it to fly to Stanstord airport near London. The men said they were fleeing persecution by the Taliban authorities in Afghanistan.

07-12-2001

The surrender of Kandahar-the last Afghan city held by the Taliban-is under way. Fighters were been giving their weapons to a commission of clerics, tribal elders and opposition commanders. Some Taliban had fled from Kandahar with their weapons. The man who was taking over as Afghan Prime minister Hamed Kharzy told the BBC they were heading for the mountains. The Americans have said their ground troops of marine commandos based nearby Kandahar intersepted Taliban convoy near the city over night and killed 7 Talibans. The surrender of the Taliban was accompanied with looting, skirmeshes and chaos.

BBC correspondent Suzanne Price reported from Quetta in Pakistan: "The Taliban forces are quitely leaving the city which they held for the past 7 years. Afghanistan's new leader Hamed Kharzy who brokered the surrender of the city said they have begun handing over their weapons. The Taliban said they would give Kandahar to a former Mujaheddin commander and his forces are already on the streets. The atmosphere is tense, shops are closed and there are few people outside their homes. The Taliban are handing over their weapons in other areas in Southern Afghanistan and the town of Spin Boldak close to the Pakistani border has been given to tribal leaders. One of the opposition commanders-a former governor of Kandahar-whose forces captured the airport, said he had not been kept informed about the talks."

As the Taliban left Kandahar the security situation there has become increasingly confused and hazardous. Rival factions have taken charge of parts of the city and an armed force remains of 3OO Arab Taliban fighters;it has been surrounded at Kandahar airport;they refused to surrender. Shooting was reported where check-points were set up.

Control of Kandahar changed hands somewhat chaotically. There have been reports of violence and looting as the Taliban withdrew and anti-Taliban forces moved in.

Other reports are of some skirmeshes between the two sides. A key question for the coalition is where is the Taliban leader Mula Mohamed Omar. The newly named leader of the interim administration in Afghanistan Hamed Kharzy who also led the fight for Kandahar said he is missing but he should be brought to justice.;that will please the Americans. But the situation in Kandahar itself is still clearly volutile;there were tension between the anti-Taliban forces with some said to be unhappy over their shares over the spoils victory and there have been already reports over clashes between some anti-Taliban groups. American planes strated bombardmets around Kandahar looking for emerging targets as a Pentagon spokeswoman put it but there was no sign of Osama ben Laden.

In Eastern Afghanistan efforts were continuing to hunt down Osama ben Laden ;there were fierce fightings in the mountainous Tura Bura area where he fled to a complex of caves occupied by hundreds of Arab fighters.

Northern Alliance units helped by US special forces attacked the caves and now control large part of it but there was no sign of Osama ben Laden. With the fall of Kandahar attention has now switched to the continuing search for Osama ben Laden-head of al Qaida network and chief suspect on the attacks on the US in September 2oo1.

There were speculations that he had retreated to a mountain fortress-a complex of caves in an area in Eastern Afghanistan known as Tura Bura occupied by hundreds of al Qaida fighters. Fighters of the Northern Alliance helped by special US forces have been attacking the complex and said they now control many of them. Electra Naysmith reported: "Throughout this 2 months miliatary campaign American officials have been careful not to identify the specific area they believed Osama ben Laden to be hiding. But just last week the head of the US Central Command general Tomy Francs confirmed that the montains South of Jalalabadwere "very interesting", as he put it. And there in ground attacks were increasingly focused on these mountainous hide-outs. Tura Bura-deep in the wild mountains is an elaborate network of caves and tunnels developed in 198Oies by anti-Soviet Afghan Mujaheddin. The underground complex is said to extend several hundred meters into the hills;equipped with power supply and ventilation systems it is told to be able to hold up to 1OOO people within its fortified walls".

Hamed Kharzy told the BBC Mula Omar was given a last chance to denounce terrorism and dissossiates from it and now after he did not made any use of this proposal he will be brought to Justice. Hamed Kharzy did not specify whether he will be broughto American or Afghan court of justice. The US defence secretary Donald Rumsfeld made it clear that the US would not accept any deal that allows Mula Omar to go free. Latest reports however said that Mula

Omar was under the protection of a local Mujaheddin commander Mula Nagibulla, who was sympathetic to the Taliban. Mula Omar was born 1959.

08-12-2001

Afghan tribal leaders occupying the Southern city of Kandahar after the Taliban surrender have formed a loca council to help end the conflicts between their rival militias;there have been armed arguments between the tribal leaders over their share of power and over the faith of the Taliban leader Mula Mohamed Omar whoo has disappeared, as BBC corresponden Peter Grester reported from Kabul the search for Mula Omar and Osama ben Laden was continuing: "They may be missing without a trace but Afghanistan's new leaders believe that of the world's most wanted men are still inside Afghanistan. The Taliban supreme leader Mula Mohamed Omar vanished as his forces handed over the last stronghold of Kandahar to the anti-Taliban factions on o7th Dec 2oo1. Although intelligence reports suggests that Osama ben Laden was hiding in Tura-Bura cave complex in the Eastern mountains, a thourough search of the captured side has found nothing. The designated leader of Afghanistan's new interim goverment Hamed Kharzy said he does not know where either man is but he is convinced that both are still inside Afghanistan".

Pakistan has stepped up surveillance of its lengthy border with Afghanistan to prevent the escape of Osama ben Laden's al Qaida network. A Pakistani spokesman said hundreds of soldiers have been deployed at key points along the border since the fall of Kandahar and armed helicopters were patrolling the area. A vital bridge linking Afghanistan with Uzbekistan which have been closed for 5 years is expected to re-open tomorrow in a new move to increase humanitarian aid across the frontier. The Uzbek President Islam Karimov said the bridge would be reopened after a final technical assesment. He was speaking at joint news conference with the visiting American Secretary of State Collin Powell who was been working at consolidating US relations in the region. Collin Powell said America is looking for a permanent change for the better in its relationship with Uzbekistan: "We are looking for relationship that will stay long after that crisis is over. I applauded Uzbekistan and the President personally for the political courage shown to assist us in this war and we will respect their courage by continuing to remain engaged with them long after the war is over".

09-12-2001

The US have carried out wave after wave of bombing raids on the Tura Bura cave complex in the Eastern mountainous region of Afghanistan. It is tought that Osama ben Laden and his supporters could be hiding there. BBC correspondent Nick Childs reported from Quetta on the Pakistani border: " As the Americans appear to be stepping up their pressure on the Tura Bura caves from the air local tribal fighters say they are preparing for a new assault on the ground with reports of reinforcements arriving by truck. One commander said Osama ben Laden was personally leading some 1OOO of his fighters in the area. Others said the al Qaida leader was in Southern Afghanistan where the hunt is also on for the Taliban leader Mula Mohamed Omar. But the coalitions 2 prime targets remain ellusive". General Richard Myers said the Americans have no absolute proof of Osama ben Lade's whereabouts but they believed he was in Tura Bura. The UN Secretary General Kofi Anan warned the US not to attack Iraq "because it will be unwise and will lead to complications". He was speaking in Oslo where he was awarded the Nobel Peace Price.

The US Vice-President Dick Chayne said American official has found a video tape in Afghanistan showing the involvement of Osama ben Laden in the September attacks on New York;the video tape was found in an abandoned house in Afghanistan. Dick Chayne restated Osama ben Laden must be handed over to a special US military court to be trialed if captured alive.

The interim leader of Afghanistan Hamed Kharzy has held talks in the Southern city of Kandahar to try to diffuse a bitter dispute between 2 rival local commanders which has led to clashes into the surrender of the last Taliban stronghold 2 days earlier. Hamed Kharzy held the talks between the former governor of Kandahar Gul Aga and his rival Mula Nagibulla who took control of Kandahar following the Taliban surrender. Hamed Kharzy told the BBC that the talks went well;further discussions were expected in the next few days.

The World Food Program said the threat of thousands of Afghans going hungry this winter was declining. A spokesman-Mike Huggins said Uzbekistan's opening of a bridge over the river on its frontier with Afghanistan meant relief supplies can now reach more people than ever before. Mike Huggins said the World Food Program was this month well ahead of its target for moving supplies into Afghanistan but were still not reaching all those it wanted to: "

We are trying to reach 6 mio people and we believe we are getting close to these toll;we are moving the food more than ever", he said. The WFPO said it has enough food stock pile to last throughout the winter.

1o-12-2001

US marines with armoured vehicles and helicopters support have moved closer to the Southern Afghan city of Kandahar as they reinforced their search for al Qaida and Taliban fighters. There have been no citings that the Taliban leader Mula Omar whose forces lost Kandahar last week but is believed to be moving around the Kandahar area with a small group of followers. Marines have been already manning roadblocks on possible escape routes in Kandahar but a spokesman said they were not planning to enter the city. Kandahar itself is reported to be tense despite a power sharing agreement between rival local commanders. The Pentagon in Washington said the US bombers have dropped daizy cutter bombs-the largest conventional weapon in the US arsenal-on the mountainous Tura Bura area of Eastern Afghanistan. That is where Osama ben Laden and other al Qaida members were believed to be hiding. A Pentagon spokesman said forces on the ground were not adle to assess the damage because of FIGHTING IN THE AREA. The deputy US defence secretary Paul Wolfowitz said many al Qaida fighters were still at large and the job to find them was likely to be very long and difficult. Meanwhile the leader of the anti-Taliban forces in the Tura Bura area said his troops had captured a strategic area about 2 km from Tura Bura.

US marines have moved back into the American Embassy in Kabul for the first time since it was abandoned 12 years ago. The marines were there to provide security for State Department officials who have come to asssess prospects for the Embassy's re-opening. The marines' arival marks the first known American military presence in Kabul where the interim goverment is due to assume power later in December 2oo1 under the UN supervised accord. However in an apparent set-back for the accord a spokesman for the Afghan defence ministry said that international peace-keepers will not be allowed to patrol the whole of the city. Correspondents said the officials' remarks indicate nervousness over the arrival of the peace keepers for it was not clear how much weight they should be given. Pakistan has reinforced its boundary with Afghanistan to prevent al Qaida fighters from crossing over into Pakistan;some 2O al Qaida fighters were captured while they crossed the border into Pakistan.

11-12-2001

There were signs that some fighters of Osama ben Laden's al Qaida network in its last big stronghold of Tura Bura were preparing to surrender. After more than a week of fighting in the mountainous Eastern region an anti-Taliban commander called the sease-fire to allow negotiations to take place. He said the al Qaida fighters would hand over their weapons tomorrow. There was no independent confirmation of this;other reports suggest there was disagreement within al Qaida command. Anti-Taliban fighters who have got into power in Tura Bura cave complex have found many bodies of al Qaida's fighters their defence oppose devasteted by intense American air raids. The groups leader Osama ben Laden was said to be leading the resistance and TRUCKLOADS OF US SOLDIERS have been seen in the area. Aid agencies said they were increasingly worried about the humanitarian situation the Southern Afghan city of Kandahar. There were no humanitarian convoys into the city for several weeks. The aid agency OXFAM said it was concerned that 6Oooo Afghans living in a make-shift camp near the Pakistani border lack food and water. Meanwhile there have been conflicting reports about the security situation in Kandahar itself. A spokesman for the city's new governer said Kandahar was calm. However local residents said looting was continuing and the Reuters news agency said hundreds of local armed men had been entering the city demanding a share in its administration. The American Secretary of State Collin Powel indicated that Britain is likely to lead an international peace-keeping force in Afghanistan. Collin Powell said a head of talks in London for the next step would be for the UN to authorize the deployment of the force. Britain said its troops were ready for a possible operation but agreement is still a long way off. Collin Powell arrived in London from Paris where the French said they were prepared to take part in an international force in Afghanistan. French officials said talks on the operation were underway with EU partners.

12-12-2001

Anti-Taliban forces in Afghanistan were still waiting to see whether fighters from Osama ben Laden's al Qaida movement will give up there mountain stronghold in the East. American bombers attacked positions in the Tura Bura area after members of al Qaida failed to meet a deadline for their surrender. BBC correspondent Peter Grester reported from Tura Bura: "There may well be talks of surrender for the al Qaida forces but on the ground there has been no sign of it happening. Instead of the expected waves of foreign al Qaida troops marching off the mountains with their hands in the air the only people to come down so far were wounded anti-Taliban fighters caught in the ongoing battle. The talk on the capitulation began on late Tuesday 11-12-2001 after the al Qaida fighters lost key defence positions lower on the Tura Bura mountains in a FIERCE BATTLE. A local commander-Hadgi Imam-said that they apparently agreed to quit at 8 o'clock on Wendesday morning local time;just before the dead line US B-52 planes underscored the time marking a GIANT FIGURE OF 8 with their verbetrals in the sky. And as the dead line passed the bombers dumped payload after payload of bombs on the mountain top filling the sky with a cloud of acred smoke and dust".

Anti Taliban commanders in Afghanistan were continuing their negotiations with al Qaida fighters who were under siege in Tura Bura cave complex. American B-52 planes used giant bombs known as green humor and daizy cutters in an attempt to flush out Osama ben Laden's fighters. But it is not clear if Osama ben Laden himself was there. His Taliban hosts were in former days controlled by the Pakistani Intelligence service-the ISI. The man who ran the ISI as the Taliban rose to power was Hamed Gul. The BBC asked him if he knew whether Osama ben Laden was in Tura Bura: "He may be there or he may be not there", he answered. "The more chances are that he is not there because Tura Bura was targeted... therefore why should be he there in case he wishes to escape arrest than he should be somewhere else in Afghanistan."

The US raised fears that Osama ben Laden may have slipped into Pakistan but Hamed Gul said he won't be a welcomed guest there: "In Pakistan the tribes may be not very sympathetic to him because tribes are very friendly with the Goverment at the moment;secondly Pakistan has a very long history of picking up any body was wanted by America and than handing them over EVEN BEYOND THE BALE OF PAKISTANI LAW. I don't think he could not take the chance of getting in to Pakistan."

The Pentagon said one of its supersonic BS1 bombers crashed into the sea near the base of Diego Garsia. All 4 crew members were killed.

A senior American offical described the complex of caves in Tura Bura area as "the last effective al Qaida stronghold" The fact that the remaining al Qaida fighters have menaged to hold out under heavy American bombing with anti-Taliban fighters advancing up the valleys is a sign of the difficulty of this terrain. The mountains always have been the strongest defence of any one resisting authority in Afghanistan. The Tura Bura caves are located in the White mountains which were among the highest peaks in this part of th country. The border with Pakistan lies among the top most ridges.

During the war against the Soviet occupation Mujaheddin fighters used remote valleys as an escape route to Pakistan and American officials fear that senior al Qaida leaders could do the same. There is no definite word of the whereabouts of the al Qaida leader Osama ben Laden but the Americans say their best guess is that HE IS in the Tura Bura region.

Pakistan sent thousands of troops to guard the border to prevent any al Qaida fighters crossing over. But apart of the harsh terrain the situation is further complicated by the fact that the Pashtoon tribes in this part of Pakistan are semi-independent and always lived according to their tribal customs. There are many supporters of the Taliban among them and some might be willing to give Osama ben Laden shelter for a time regardless of the wishes of the Pakistani goverment. But if he is here and if his escape is impossible it is quite likely that Osama ben Laden and his most comitted followers will simply fight to the death. They know they can expect no mercy from the enemy who surround them.

At the other end of the country the Taliban's former stronghold of Kandahar is now returning to some resemblence of normal life;the Taliban surrendered the city a week earlier after negotiations with the new interim leader Hamed Kharzy.

On an enormous vulcanic outcrop known as Elephant's mountain the Taliban anti aircraft defences remain intact. There is a large green and yellow painted mosque built on Osama ben Laden's orders as gift for Mula Omar. The assumption is the special forces are helping guaranty Hamed Kharzy's security and participating in the search for Mula Omar and Osama ben Laden.

The US Attorney General John Ashcroft has hold talks in London with the British Home Secretary David Blunket on NEW LEGAL MEASURES to combat terrorism. Britain is the first stop of John Ashcroft's tour of Europe where he will be holding with law-inforcement officials on legal means to curb Osama ben Laden's al Qaida network. The German Government has banned 2O Islamist groups that it calls extremists. The main one is a Cologne based organization the Khalifat State whose aim is to establish a theocratic state in Turkey. German authorities have also carried out house searches at some 2OO premises including a number of mosques. The action is one of the largest in Europe in persuit of radical Muslim groups since September suicide attacks in the US. The German interior minister Otto Schilly announced the ban on the Khalifate of Cologn and related organizations. The ban and wide spread police searches followed a new law in removing the groups protection. The Khalifate is one of the most outspokenly agressive Islamist organizations in Europe comitted to the overthrow of the secular goverment in Turkey. Turkish community leaders warned that overzealous police actions in the name of security WILL HARM RACE RELATIONS. But the German Goverment said it was investigating possible links between the Khalifate and Osama ben Laden's al Qaida network.

Afghanistan's foreign minister desifnate Abdula Abdula began a 2 days visit to India for talks with Prime minister Atar Bahari Vachpeh and other key politicians. A spokesma for the goverment in Delhi said Mr. Abdula's trip high-lighted the important role India had to play in the reconstruction of Afghanistan.

13-12-2001

The head of Afghanistan's interim administration Hamed Kharzy has been meeting members of his new cabinett in Kabul. It is Hamed Kharzy's first time in the Afghan capital since he was appointed by fellow Afghans at a meeting in Bonn. He also held talks with the former President Burhanudin Rabani. Mr. Kharzy told the BBC the talks were friendly. He reiterated a call for international forces to deploy in the country ahead of his official swearing in on 23rd December. Mr. Kharzy denounced the housted Taliban regime saying it had destroyed the values of Afghanistan. US aircraft have resumed heavy attacks on the Tura Bura area in Eastern Afghanistan after the deadline passed with no sign of al Qaida fighters agreeing to a conditional surrender. As American planes bombed mountain positions held by al Qaida fighters local anti-Taliban commanders said they had given up attempts to negotiate.

A video tape has been released by the US goverment which it sais shows compelling evidence that Osama ben Laden knew in advance about the attacks in New York and Washington on 11th September. The video tape was found in Jalalabad.

In the 1 hour long video tape transmitted by the CNN relaxed and cheerful Osama ben Laden is seen discussing how the attacks were planned. Osama ben Laden in a white turban and deep-grey jacket is sitting cross-legged on the floor of a bare room with 3 other men. They chat and laugh recalling the events of 11th September. The sound is muffled but something is clear- Osama ben Laden sais he knew the exact timing of the attacks 5 days before they happened but adds grinning that the high-jackers themselves did not know this was a suicide mission.

He describes listening the news on the radio on being delighted that destruction of the World Trade Center in New York was far more devastating than he had expected. He explains to his companions that some of those who had carried out the suicide attacks were only told the details of the operation in the last moment. The POOR QUALITY TAPE is said to be found by American intelligence officers in Afghanistan. A BBC correspondent in Washington said President Bush took the decision to release the tape in the hope that it would convince American allies of Osama ben Laden's guilt. Britain sais the video tape leaves no room for doubt about the involvement of Osama ben Laden in the 11th September attacks. A spokesman for the Prime Minister Tony Blair said there was also no doubt about authenticity of the tape. A senior member of the US Congress Senator Richard Shelby said "it offered damning evidence of Osama ben Laden's complicity". Atah Abdul Gawa-a Washington journalist-said: "In certain moments I have the doubt this words are coming from Osama ben Laden's lips". The biographer of Osama ben Laden Hamed Mir said "this tape was deliberately left by Osama ben Laden to make the Pentagon broadcast it across the world". Many Arab journalists said the tape was faked; others said it was at least manipulated. TheTaliban defence minister said Osama ben Laden cannot be so naive to say such things on a record.

But a leading Saudi dissident in London said the tape was genuine because of its topic. The UAE information minister said it was authentic. The tape has been called "ben Laden's smoking gun" and its releasing has been contraversial but the White House hopes that the sight of Osama ben Laden will consolidate support among the Arab nations.

In Afghanistan US bombers and Afghan militia fighters have stepped up their efforts to captire Tura Bura the last substential stronghold controlled by Osama ben Laden's al Qaida movement. A BBC correspondent near Tura Bura said that despite air and ground attacks and bad weather the al Qaida fighters were putting up strong resistence.

The defenders of Tura Bura have refused an offer of protection if they surrendered. A local militia commander-Hasrat Ali-said that he believed that many of the al Qaida leaders who are believed to be at Tura Bura had fled the area but that he hope to capture alive any who remained.

14-12-2001

American air and ground forces have stepped up their activity in the Tura Bura area in Eastern Afghanistan amidst reports that Osama ben Laden may be hand in there with hundreds of his al Qaida fighters. Reports have say heavy bombing over night and again after down has forced al Qaida fighters to abandon some of their positions and take cover in caves. More American special forces have been sent to the area to take part in the fightings. The US said the fierceness of the fighting reporting citings by anti-Taliban forces and intelligence information all pointing to Osama ben Laden being in the Tura Bura area. The American aircraft have been supported by an increased number of SPECIAL FORCES on the ground. Sources at the Pentagon said they believed Osama ben Laden may still be in the area. BBC correspondent Damian Grammaticus has been watching the bombing and reported about the devastating supremacy of the Americans.

Meanwhile American marines have taken control of the heavily damaged airport outside the Taliban stronghold of Kandahar; when repaired the airport will be handed over to new Afghan authorities and there is hope that food aid will be delivered more easily. BBC correspondent Suzanne Price reported from Quetta across the border with Pakistan: "A week after the Taliban surrendered Kandahar city the American marines are now moving in. A convoy travelled to the area and cut off routes as more marines were brought in by helicopters. Officials said they will clear the airport of any booby traps or mines and bring in air traffic controllers. They said part of the runway was still usable and they can bring in some cargo planes. However there are still many large bomb craters as well as shrapnel and debory scattered round the area. The Americans said they will hire local contracters to help rebuild the airport which can be also used to bring in international humanitarian aid".

All 15 EU countries agreed to contribute EU multinational peace keeping force which to take part in international peace force in Afghanistan. The news was given at the EU summit at Laaken near Brussels. Military officials from several EU countries together with the USA, Jordan and Turkey held a separate meeting in London to discuss the formation of the Afghan force. It is hope that the first elements of this force will be in place in Kabul when the Afghan interim goverment takes office in just over a week's time. The defence minister of the interim goverment Mohamed Fahim said he does not want a force larger than a 1OOO men. 1Oooo anti-war protesters surrounded Laaken to protest against the escalation of the war in Afghanistan. Police used water cannons and DOGS to disperse the protesters which braved the bitter cold of minus 5 degrees. MEP Caroline Stuart joined the protesters in an anti-war demonstration.

The yesterday released hour long video tape was watched by thousands of people round the world;some Arab commentators doubted the AUTHENTICITY OF THE TAPE. BBC correspondent in Islamabad Suzane Price said "it is a common view here that the tape is a fake manufactured by the Americans". But in Afghanistan itself televisions are rare.

BBC correspondent Ion McWilliam was in Kabul where he was gaging reactions: "American officials said the video was proof that the chief suspect Osama ben Laden was responcible for the attacks on 11th September.

Most people in Kabul DO NOT HAVE THE SATELITE DISHES nessecary to receive international TV channels. But foreign radio stations broadcasting in Persian and Pashtoon chiefly the BBC are widely listened to and important news generally spread quickly by the word of mouth. Even so many people in Kabul have yet not heard of the video. And there is SOME SCEPTICISM among those who have. It is a common view in Afghanistan that Osama ben Laden was simply not powerful enough to organize the attacks on New York from his Afghan hide-away. Taliban opposers think Osama ben Laden had close contacts with international terrorists and may have been responsible for the World Trade Center attacks;but those who think he WAS NOT RESPONSIBLE won't be nessecarily be convinced by this video. Most people here are pre-ocupied with the return to normal life after the Taliban's departure and are getting ready for the eat festival after the end of Ramadan today when day-time fasting will end. Even while the search for Osama ben Laden continues in Eastern Afghanistan and bombing continues round Tura Bura the events in New York 3 months ago are not the main concern in Kabul".

President Bush said the video tape of Osama ben Laden released yesterday amounts to a devastating admission of guilt for the attacks against New York and Washington on 11th September. Speaking in Washington Mr. Bush said it was preposterous that any one could think THE TAPE HAVE BEEN FAKED by the Americans. He said, "it was a feeble excuse to provide weak support for an evil man." The President repeated his determination to get Osama ben Laden: "It might be tomorrow, in a month or in a year", he said "but we will get him". And he again said he did not care if he was dead or alive.

But in Newshour at 21:2O GMT Judy Swallow said Osama ben Laden knew of the attacks 4 days in advance while yesterday's message was Osama ben Laden knew 5 days in advance. Audio forensic expert Dr. Peter French said the present level of science and technic allows the tape to be doctored;it could be the latest Hollywood achievement. How could Osama ben Laden know of the attacks and the CIA not supposed that his phone was permanently bugged?

Abdul Aturak-a translator of an Arab newspaper-said there were gaps in the translation and the translation itself was inaccurate.

15-12-2001

The Americans said their special forces and Afghan allies were engaged in a grim fight against Osama ben laden's al Qaida movement in the mountainous Tura Bura region of Afghanistan. The US defence secretary Donald Rumsfeld said being in Azerbaijan "a very energetic battle was under way". A local militia commander Hadgi Zahir said important peaks were captured over night;with the coming of day light B-52 bombers resumed their attacks on al Qaida positions. The Americans said some al Qaida members were captured and will be interrogated;they did not show the captured fighters on TV. BBC correspondent in Tura Bura Damian Grammaticus reported: "Several hours after al Qaida and Taliban fighters had apparently offered to surrender there was no sign of any of them handing in their weapons. A local commander from the Eastern Shura forces fighting alongside with the Americans said he believes it may have been a diversion designed to allow to al Qaida men to flee. Small groups were attempting to escape by riding donkeys over the high mountain passes towards Pakistan. Of the main target-Osama ben Laden-there was still no sign. Hazrat Ali-leading the ground assault said Osama ben Laden may be trapped in a cave with a 100 of his men. The Americans though admit they do not know where Osama ben Laden is." Donald Rumsfeld held talks in Azerbaijan as part of the mission to bolster the US coalition against Afghanistan. Mr. Rumsfeld said the US is grateful for Azerbaijan's continuing support ofr the campaign and that he hoped the two countries would enjoy closer military cooperation. Mr. Rumsfeld was going to Armenia and will travel on to Georgia and Uzbekistan.
< IRAQ . TXT >

10 JAN 2003 35000 US troops sent to The Gulf
11 JAN 2003 27000 US troops sent to The Gulf
20 JAN 26000 UK troops & 120 tanks
21 JAN 37000 US troops
15 FEB 2003 150 000 US troops estimated
09-09 2003 10 500 British troops in Iraq plus 2 new bataillons to send

The American desire is from the Northern front in Turkey to distroy Iraq: finally this plan failed and the American invasion began from the South.

< IRAQ-E1.TXT >
In a special BBC-Interview today 20 Nov at 10:00 GMT the Iraqi representative Mustafa Adami said: " Not Iraq but the USA posses weapons of mass distruction; and not only posses them but also used them in Hiroshima and in Vietnam and in Iraq used depleted uranium. On the concience of the US Presidents lay the death of 1 700 000 peaceful Iraqi civilists

who died from starvation and radiation in the years after the Golf war 1991. In Yugoslavia-not in Kosovo-the Amricans didn't hesitate to bombard kindergartens, hospitals, senior homes, embassies and TV-stations". After this words Mustafa Adami was interrupted by the BBC-moderator Elizabeth Doucet who speaks with a sharp voice and stinging brogue-accent.

Also on BBC on 19 NOV at 15:00 GMT the Bulgarian journalist Iwo Indzhew praised the new-comers to the NATO. Iwo Indzhew, who has rather weak voice and rather bad English boasted himself to be a comentator at the Bulgarian Television BTV. He praised the newcomers to the NATO-club with the following example: " When an ill man goes to the dentist he goes not for love to the dentist but because he needs him for his treatment". Iwo Indzhev failed to elaborate if the new comers do need such a "dentist" and how expensive such a depleting medication will coast to the news comers. He failed to compare the also with Austria and with Switzerland, who do existist already 53 years without the NATO-"therapy".

< IRAQ . TXT >
10 JAN 2003 35000 US troops sent to The Gulf
11 JAN 2003 27000 US troops sent to The Gulf
20 JAN 26000 UK troops & 120 tanks
21 JAN 37000 US troops
15 FEB 2003 150 000 US troops estimated
09-09 2003 10 500 British troops in Iraq plus 2 new bataillons to send

The American desire is from the Northern front in Turkey to distroy Iraq: finally this plan failed and the American invasion began from the South.

< IRAQ-E1.TXT >
In a special BBC-Interview today 20 Nov at 10:00 GMT the Iraqi representative Mustafa Adami said: " Not Iraq but the USA posses weapons of mass distruction; and not only posses them but also used them in Hiroshima and in Vietnam and in Iraq used depleted uranium. On the concience of the US Presidents lay the death of 1 700 000 peaceful Iraqi civilists who died from starvation and radiation in the years after the Golf war 1991. In Yugoslavia-not in Kosovo-the Amricans didn't hesitate to bombard kindergartens, hospitals, senior homes, embassies and TV-stations". After this words Mustafa Adami was interrupted by the BBC-moderator Elizabeth Doucet who speaks with a sharp voice and stinging brogue-accent.

Also on BBC on 19 NOV at 15:00 GMT the Bulgarian journalist Iwo Indzhew praised the new-comers to the NATO. Iwo Indzhew, who has rather weak voice and rather bad English boasted himself to be a comentator at the Bulgarian Television BTV. He praised the newcomers to the NATO-club with the following example: " When an ill man goes to the dentist he goes not for love to the dentist but because he needs him for his treatment". Iwo Indzhev failed to elaborate if the new comers do need such a "dentist" and how expensive such a depleting medication will coast to the news comers. He failed to compare the also with Austria and with Switzerland, who do existist already 53 years without the NATO-"therapy".

< SADDAM. TXT >

13 December 2OO3 at O3:OO Iraqi time: Arrest of Saddam Hussein:

13 December 2OO3 at O3:OO EET :

Paul Bremer, US-administrator to Iraq said to the media: "Ladies and Gentlemen we got'm". His picture was shawn to the world despite the Geneva convention to protect prisoners of war agains public curiosity. But the USA seem to be in a long-standing breach of all conventions it has signed in recent years. In Iraq the American occupation forces succeeded finally in capturing the former dictator Saddam Hussein at O8:26 local time in Al Dawr-15 km from his native Northern town Tikrit where he was hiding in a small building; he was presented to the media, looking very exhausted and unshaven.

DNA-tests were taken to confirm he was really Saddam Husein. Nevertheless Iraqi resistance didn't stop, a bomb exploded in the town of Khandiliya near Baghdad, killing one Iraqi. An American expert waskilled when he tried to release a bomb by a controlled explosion when he tried to dispose a suspected device. In another incident 17 Iraqis were kiled by another suicide bomb attack near Bghdad. On the background of Saddam's capture Afghan news faded away for some time.

Saddam "will face justice ... but how and when is still before us", an American spokesman said. The French foreign minister de Villepain said, "the news of the capture of Saddam Hussein is a very good news!".

The operation of capturing Saddam Hussein was called "Red Dawn", 6OO US soldiers participated in it:they hit in 2 locations: Wulfering-1 and Wulfering-2 on the banks of the Tigris-river, he was moving from one place to another every 4 hours. No communication devices were found with him, reported CNN-correspondent in Iraq Nic Robertson, so he cannot been able to direct any suicide or bomb attack on US-troops in Iraq. Saddam Hussein underwent a medical examination and is in "good health", so "he can stay a fair trial, a public trial".

German Chancellor Gerhard Schroeder congratulated US-president George W. Bush "with the success of the operation", the spokeswomen of the French President Chirack did the same: "The capture of Saddam Hussein will contribute to peace, security and democracy in Iraq", he said.

The German foreign minister Joschka Fischer said: "Saddam was arrested with a full right, now he'll be brought to justice as soon as possible", his sons Udai and Kusei were killed by the Americans in April 2OO3. Saddam Hussein became awkward to the West after he defied not to recognize in 199O the border of Kuwait drown up earlier by the British. The arrest of Saddam Hussein was an important step into pacification and normalization of Iraq. "Saddam will face the justice he denied to millions in his former ruling; I congratulate the US-forces for their bravery", President George W. Bush said in TV-interview.

The message of Saddam's arrest was pronounced by Paul Bremer, civil US-administrator of Iraq: "Ladies and Gentlmen, we got'm", he said to the media and was applauded by them. Now Americans are confident that the attacks against them will collapse although no communication devices were captured with Saddam Hussein from which was possible to conclude that Saddam was directly commanding the attacks on American targets.

"The capture of Saddam Hussein doesn't mean stop of violence in Iraq, we have to capture'm one by one", US-president George W. Bush said in a TV-interview to Euronews. But only 1 hour later a mighty bomb exploded in a Baghdad hotel. Another suicide bomb attack hit an Iraqi police station killing 17 Iraqis and a gun fire to a benzine-reservoir caused it to catch fire. 2 other American convoys were shot at and bombed down near Kuwait-city. The arrest of former dictator Sddam Hussein was announced also by US-president George W. Bush: "He was arrested in a farm house near Tikrit, were he was on his hiding. No casualties were given during his arrest;he was arrested without a single shot", President Bush said in TV speech: "Now he'll face justice", Bush added. With him were found a gun, 2 Kalashnikows AK-47 and 750 000 $ in cash; "now he'll not escape justice", President Bush added.

"He hadn't even the guts to kill himself", another officious BBC-correspondent said in order to flutter the US-cowboys. One way or another the captur of Saddam Hussein, whose head have been prised by 25 000 000 USD, is a great success for the US-forces occupiyng Iraq;they've been futile in the past 8 months of their cruel occupation of Iraq in 2003. "Christmass will be gloryful for president George W. Bush", another officious correspondent claimed on the day of his capture. The problems behind his arrest will remain for the History and for the generatins to come. Saddam Hussein was a honest and staunch supporter of many peoples and countries in the World, whom he supplied with cheap oil; Saddam was instrumental in the US-attack on Iran but he was never paid the dividents of his support the USA in its war against Iran. Now Saddam will be trialed by a special tribunal-"fair and open and he will be able to call witnesses", but Saddam faces possibly the dead penalty and he will be executed-in my opinion-in May or June 2004. UN-Secretary General Kofi Annan called the move "infortunate" and added "the UNO is against his dead penalty".

No sympathy from no hook of the world will be able to spare Saddam afront the US-might and pressure for justice despite the fact no biological, no chemical and no atomic weapons were found in Iraq during the American occupation of Iraq starting in April 2003 and with no outlooks to finish even in 2005. This turbulent development with captured Sdadam Hussein will certainly overshadow the Halliburton affair with misuse of American public and military fonds and Halliburton-a friendly company to US-president George W. Bush-will may have forgotten its recent financial manipulations to the Pentagon and to US-military. "Many Arab journalist cheered, screamed with delight and called "death to Saddam Hussein", an Arab woman journalist said to the CNN from Al Arabiya-the Pentagon sponsored Arabic TV station: "Good for George W. Bush in his starting re-election campaign, good for the Arab world", she said further to the CNN in an Al Arabiya extract. Saddam is expected by the US-command to impend further attacks on Americans", was stated to the CNN. A word was spoken-for the first time-on Arab Mudjahiddin or Arab freedom-fighters very much alike to the Afghan Mujahiddin.

"The capture of Saddam doesn't mean stop of the violence in Iraq", President George W. Bush boasted to the media when 2 US-military convoys were attacked already the same day separately in the outskirts of Kuwait city. During his arrest Saddam Hussein did no resistance although he had 2 Kalashnikovs AK-47 and a handgun. He simply said in English: "I am

Saddam Hussein: I am president of Iraq and I want to negotiate!". US-president George W. Bush said, 'it's a good news and Saddam will receive fair trial under international scrutiny but it is up to the Iraqi people to decide if Saddam will receive the death penalty!". So from the very beginning George W. Bush flunged his weight after the death penalty for Saddam Hussein.

There is no doubt the arrest of Saddam Hussein is a major boost for George W. Bush's reelection campaign in November 2004 and Bush is playing this card : "I'll continue to protect our country whatsoever the price;a free and peaceful Iraq is part of protection of America", Bush said to the media. The arrest of Saddam Hussein is a good news for Bush and he will play this card untill the presidential elections in November 2004. Saddam will be trialed for failing to comply with US-foreign policy, for his Middle-East policy and for his support of the Palestinian cause for independent Palestinian state but also for refusing to hand down the Iraqi vast oil reserves-2nd in the world-to the Americans. Angry students in his native town of Tikrit organized a big demonstration to protest against his arrest which has come short of international juridical standards: " Slobodan Milosevic was treated better", the media said. Many Americans feel that after no weapons of mass destruction were found-which was the pretext of the Iraq war-no war at all should be fought. Many dictators in Latin America tramp down human rights with their feet-but since they serve American interests-no actions are taken against them for their staunch service to US-interests. When Iraq produced a 11.000 pages report on Iraqi's weapons of mass destruction the original was stollen, hidden and handed to the US by the Venezuelan president, who held presidency of the UN than. The other UN-member countries got only a censured and editted copy of this report-alms and pittance of the Americans to them. One way or another President Saddam Hussein will face the death penalty with no mercy-the USA will find enough willing witnesses and judges for this show trial just ahead of the presidential reelection campaign of George W. Bush in November 2004. Syrian president Bashir el Assad called the capture of Saddam Hussein "an internal Iraqi matter".

The news of Saddam's capture made a boost also to share markets: British shares rose by 3.25%. American officials said Saddam will meat the judgement of its own Iraqi people. With Saddam in American hands, Americans will not let him go any time. Americans suggest Saddam must face justice of his own people, to be judged by the Provisional Goverment not to be introduced to an international tribunal. No communication devices were found with Saddam, so he was giving moral not tactical support to his people. X-mas has come early for American President Bush and is an enormous boost for his reelection campaign in 2004. "Germany was a stanch supporter of America in its Afghanistan war;so German companies maybe finally electable for reconstruction contaracts in Iraq", Bush said. The capture of Saddam only inspired new suicide bomb attacks in Husseiniya and in Ramadi and in Amariya-district in Baghdad: "Saddam is a world hero", the crowds chanted and the killings went on in suicide attacks showing loyalty to Saddam Hussein, who was President of Iraq for over 2 decades.

Demonstrations of angry Saddam's supporters took place in Fallujah, Ramadi and in Saddam's native town of Tikrit and officious Iraqi police had no other choice but to diperse the demonstrators by tear gas and rubber buttons injuring many of them but they manifestated their readiness and willingness to return to the old terms of living rather than to give up to the Americans.

Saddam Hussein was born in Tikrit on 29th April 1937 in a very poor family. Attended a bomb attack which failed so he fled to Cairo and studied law. There the Americans hired him as a CIA-agent. He arried his girl-cousin and had 2 boys and 3 girls from her. Appointed to President by the former Iraqi President and thus betrayed his former socialist program. Urged and supporte by the Americans invaded Iran and 1990 Quawait. Celebrated in 1992 when President George Bush senior lost the elections. In the 1995-plebescit only 3000 people voted "NO". In a time of a crisis he never slept more than 3 hours and he moved from place to place. Revered by so many, Saddam's ruling will not be forgotten, CNN said. Tony Blair was very reserved and thanked to the Americans for capturing Saddam Hussein: "It is a new chance for the Iraqi people", he said to the media. Israeli prime minister Ariel Sharon phoned his colleague George W. Bush to thank him for the capture of Saddam Hussein. In Gaza the news of Saddam's capture was met with sorrow. Saddam paid 10.000$ to the families of those killed in the intifiada, smaller summes to the wounded. Saddam was born in a mud-hut in Tikrit and he was deeply ignorent of the world abroad, CNN-journalists mocked at him-but only a f t e r he was captured. The USA expects from him now to reveal more details of the Iraqi nuclear, biological and chemical weapon program-which I suspect deeply will bring the US to nothing but a strifle and mutual accuses of institutions. "Saddam was caught just like a rat", said Ray Odierno-Major General, Commander of 4th US infantry Division in Iraq.

Now Saddam-aged 66-will suffer many more indignities in American prisons. Saddam was betrayed by some one of his friends, greedy for the US-award of 25.000.000 USD. The 4th infantry division was for 10 days after him, when a a close assosiate betrayed him, said General Ray Odierno to the media. Now in prison, Saddam may think over who actually betrayed him. Iraq since long had become a clogue-mire, CNN asserted. "This is end of the road for Saddam", George W. Bush declared this ominous day. The International Red Cross Commitee protested against this public humiliation which is in breach of Geneva convention-no Saddam-pictures should be publisized to avoid embarrassement and humiliation of him. George Bush denied he was using the publicity to boost his reelection campaign in 2004-a long way ahead to see what will happen to other presidents too.

In The Hague General Wesley Clark started to give evidence against the former president of Yugoslavia Slobodan Milosevic-behind of closed doors for security reasons. General Wesley Clark, who led the US-bomb operation against civilian Yugoslav targets in spring 1999 is also contestor in the US-presidential elections in November 2004. At police stations in Husseiniya and in Ramadi suicide bombs exploded tearing 11 into death. "If America believes the capture of Saddam will pacify the Iraq-this is the result-suicide bombings on a large scale. Saddam is one of the world's heroes and time will not bleach his national image especially after a call for an international tribunal", wrote an Arab newspaper. Many Iraqi protested against his arrest and demonstrated their willingness to come back to the elder conditions of life. In Ramadi and in

Tikrit-Saddam's native town-officious Iraqi police had had no other choice but to disperse the angry demonstrants with tear gas and rubber sticks.

14 DEC 2003

An assessination attempt was made on the Pakistani President Pervez Musharraf when his car convoy approached the city of Rawalpandi a bomb exploded alongside the road. Rawalpandi is head quarters of the Pakistani Army only few miles South from the Capital Islamabad so General Musharraf uses the road on a daily basis. Only few words were mentioned on this assessination attempt because it was overshadowed by the capture of the Iraqi dictator Saddam Hussein.

15 December 2003:

US-Secretary of state Colin Powell underwent a surgery operation for prostate cancer. The Secretary's said to be well after the operation which was different from his armed operations in Iraq and in Afghanistan which did cost the lives of so many civilians. It was not said whether Colin Powell will undergo chemotherapy or blood transfusion to survive after the operation. 3 mighty explosions rocked the Afghan Capital Kabul;one of the explosions was close to the airport. No reports on casualties are made as details are still coming in. The next day massive demonstrations against Saddam's capture broke out in Fallujah, Ramadi, Tikrit, Mosul, Samarra and Baghdad.

The Americans opened fire at the demonstrators and killed 11 of them only in Samarra. In Samarra rocket-propelled grenades were fired at the Americans.

17 December 2003

A suicide driver drove his vehicle packed with explosives into a mini bus in the center of Baghdad killing 22 people. Iniatially he meant to attack the nearby police station. Now terrorists prefer soft targets such as civilians and police stations and not heavily fortified military bases. Later this day the US-military refuted its own statement, saying it was not a suicide attack but a traffic accident in which a fuel-truck hit a full-packed passenger mini-bus. Finally Lyse Doucet too added her voice to the officious American version-how can a day pass without her reports! In Samarra American soldiers arrested 73 Iraqis accusing them to be supporters of Saddam Hussein. In Samarra many Iraqi died in uprising against the Americans in the begin of December and only yesterday 11 new were killed in Samarra. A sharp rise in Dutch unemployment was reported by Euronews-447 OOO are out of job-the highest figure ever in Holland. It is 250% of the 196 OOO unemployed expected in January 2OO3. Steven Kenny-an Australian lawyer-was allowed to visit the Guantanamo prison camp. He described it as "a whole black hole, where basic rights are denied to the prisoners", BBC said.

18 December 2003

The Arabic TV-Station al Jezzera distributed a video-casette of the second high in the Afghan command saying "the Americans were inable to potect themselves. No reason to spare them all over the world." The US-administrator of Iraq Paul Bremer admitted, he'd narrowly escaped an attack by Iraqi militants on 06 December 2003 when a bomb exploded alongside the road when his vehicle was passing along.

19 December 2003

The American troops in Iraq shot dead 3 Iraqi policemen and wounded 3 further. They said, they have taken mistakenly for bandits and opened fire at them. The US-authorities in Iraq said, they will launch an investigation in the case. Since the end of the war over 100 Iraqi policemen lost their lives either in ambushes of Saddam's loyalists or by mistaken American fire. At the same time the German Chansellor Gerhard Schroder said, he is principally against any death penalty, including this one of the captured Iraqi dictator Saddam Hussein.

21 December 2003

The delegates for the Loya Jirga-the Afghan National Assembley-came together and discussed the plans for new constitution and for elections in June 2004 amidst heavy security. In Iraq loyalists to Saddam Hussein set afire several pipe lines near Tikrit-the home town of Saddam. In Baghdad the loyalist attacked with rockets a tank depot in one part of the city and set ablaze a huge fuel reservoir in another one causing even more fuel shortages;the present fuel price is 30 Dinar a liter. Americans arrested in Baghdad more than 100 loyalists to Saddam and interrogated them-with small results-they said. In the area near the Syrian border 60 further Iraqi loyalists were arrested and interrogated, said 1st lt. Brian Joyce to the BBC. He didn't reveal the kind of information, US-military received from that particular Chrismas interrogations.

Saddam Hussein himself was also interrogated but the Americans said he were absolutely not cooperative to them. No lawyer has been allocated to him since his arrest 8 days earlier on 13-12-2003 when American and Iraqi Christians prepare to celebrate Christmas. An outcry became louder for a reconciliation commission South African style.

The Spanish Prime minister Josni Maria Aznar inspected the Spanish troops in Iraq and stood with them for a short dinner but than retreated hastily losing no single word on Saddam, on his conditions and on his chance of a lawyer. Saddam is expected to accuse the Americans for urging him into the 8-yeasr war with Iran in the 1980ies.

At the war crime tribunal in The Hague general Wesley Clark testified again against the former Yugoslavian President Slobodan Milosevic who is imprisoned already 3 years. Milosevic said nothing to his accusations but took a notice into his small paper-block in front of him. General Wesley Clark is Democratic candidate for the forthcoming US-Presidential elections in November 2004 and hopes to boost by his testimony his chances for an US-president in the presidential run-up. On 28 December 2003 during the Serbian elections the Serbian Democratic President Woislaw Kostunica who has chance to be reelected, said to Euronews at 20:04 & 20:34 CET : "The Tribunal in The Hague is a threat to stability". In later editions Euronews removed his remark from broadcasting.

In Washington the US-head of Homeland Security, raised the allert to the stage of orange "high" in front of expected terrorist attacks against the USA. Tom Ridge said the USA are under threat of terrorist attacks for the Christmas days and increased the alarm level to "orange"-the second-higher one. Pope John Paul II called for calm and peace in the forthcoming celebration days; now nobody is sure when where and how Al Qaida will hit the next American target. Since long time Al Qaida has no interest-or no means-to hit Americans in Afghanistan any more since there are so many soft targets in the Middle East.

13 Israeli soldiers had signed an open letter to their prime minister Ariel Sharon and to their defence minister refusing to serve in the Israeli army at the Gaza strip "where the human rights of the Palestinians are tramp down; serving in such an army is disgraceful, shameful and morbid to Israel's image at home and abroad", they wrote. They've received no answer to their letter yet.

22-12-2003

A side bomb exploded in Baghdad killing 2 Americans and a translator. The Egyptian foreign minister Ahmed Mahad has been treated in hospital after been attacked by Palestinian protesters at Al Aksa-Mosque in Jerusalem the 3rd most holy sight in Islam. Witnesses said a group of Palestinian protesters threw shoes at the Minister and accused'm of being a traitor. Israeli police (?) said to've entered the compound surrounding the mosque and helped the Minister Egyptian body-guards half-pull half-carry him out, said the BBC-Jerussalem correspondent Jill MacGibery: "Soon aterwards Israeli police officers rushing into the mosque half pool half-carrying'm out. Mr. Mahad looked ushered and distressed. his hand at his throat. Israeli police said his attackers had posed him with shoes, which is a Muslim derrogative sign. Mr. Mahad was treated by medics nearby: he doesn't seem to be seriously injured in the attack:he was described as fully conscience throughout". The Egyptian President Hosni Moubarag called the incident deeply regretable". Russia agreed to ride off 66% of Iraqi debts to it-8 billion USD.

24 December 2003

A mighty explosion ripped the Iraqi Capital Baghdad killing 3 US-soldiers. Skirmeshes occurred also in other parts of Baghdad, at least 1OO Iraqis were injured. Saddam's loyalists fired a rocket at Sheraton Hotel in Baghdad late in the night. The hotel rocked but no casualties were reported.

The French Air lines Air France cancelled 6 flights from Paris to Los Angeles after a request of the American Embassy in Paris, which said it received information of possible Al Qaida attacks: "An Al Qaida agent has infiltrated Air France", the Embassy claimed. A case of mad cow disease in the USA shook additionally the American image abroad. The top importers of American beef Japan, Mexico and South Korea imposed immediately ban on all American beef followed by Taiwan, Russia, Ukraine, Malaysia, Singapore, Hong Kong, South Africa, Columbia, Chili. Canada imposed a partial ban. In his traditional Christmas mess Pope John Paul II called the American aggression in Iraq "shameful" and urged them to stop the blood shed.

25 December 2003

President Musharraf of Pakistan had narrowly survived an attempt on his life-the second in 11 days;the Dutch RTL TV said it was the 3rd attack on his life when a road side bomb exploded in the garrisson city of Rawalpindi when the presidential convoy drove along. Suicide bombers attacked his convoy close to the army head quarters in Rawalpindi. President Musharraf was said afterwards to be safe but the Pakistani interior minister told reporters that at least 14 people were killed. The BBC-correspondent in Islamabad Paul Anderson, said this latest attempt to kill President Musharraf was sophisticated coordinated and very close. Two suicide bombers in pick-up trucks packed with explosives pulled out of separate petrol stations and drove into president Musharraf's convoy as it passed. One of them hit but not the president's armoured limousine, the second one menaged to hit it from behind. Most of those killed and injured were passers-by. The attack happened close to the bridge which bombers blew up 11 days earlier only few seconds after the president's convoy had passed. Pakistani officials refused to comment on who might be behind the attack but suspicion will fall first on Islamic extremists angry with the president for his support for the United States. A suspicion was spoken out that the attacks were organized by some one of Musharraf's inner circle who knews exactly his travel schedules. "It's a full failure of the intelligence gathering service", said the Pakistani information minister Sheikh Rashid Ahmed. Several hours after the suicide detonation president Musharraf appeared on TV showing that he's healthy and intact: "we don't know yet who is behind the attack but shall trace them down", he said in a TV address to the nation; only one day earlier he promised to step down as Army leader dissolving a raw with the Islamist opposition which had virtually paralyzed the goverment. But such concessions are unlikely to blokade militant extremists who are furrious on his alliance with the US-war on terrorism. They are even angrier on measures which General Musharraf took against his own ranks recently.

General Pervez Musharraf assumes that al Qaida could be behind the first assessination bid on him only 11 days earlier on the same road just before a bridge. The previous assessination attempt on president Musharraf took place on 14th December 2003 on the same road connecting the Capital Islam abad with the military head quarters Rawalpindi. The city of Rawalpindi is the head quarters of the Pakistani Army and it is very close to the capital Islamabad so general Musharraf uses the road between the 2 cities almost daily. This is the second attempt on his life, the Dutch RTL-TV asserted at 23:45 this were the third attempt.

In Baghdad several rockets were fired by guerrillas at American targets including also on Hotel Sheraton where many Westerners are accomodated; this is the second attack on the Sheraton hotel in 2 days. In a town near Tel Avive a suicide bomber killed 4 Israelis and wounded 18 others at a bus stop. Israelis killed in their turn high-ranking Palestinian Commanders in a helicopter-rocket attack at the Gaza-strip

26 December 2003

2 American soldiers were killed in a rocket attack in the Iraqi town Baquba. Further 5 American soldiers died when they were trying to difuse a home-made bomb in Baghdad. The attacks on Americans had subsided recently to 17 a day but only today and alone in Baghdad there were reported 26 attacks on Americans, the media said.

27 December 2003

The Bulgarian goverment confirmed officially 4 Bulgarian soldiers were killed and 15 further injured in 3 coordinated car bombs, mortars and machine guns' attacks in Kerbala-110 km southwest from Baghdad. 2 Thai and 7 Iraqi soldiers were also killed in the attacks while further 35 coalition soldiers were injured. Up to 130 Iraqi civilians were also injured including the governor of Kerbala, which are now in city hospitals for treatment, reported from Baghdad the BBC-correspondent Chris Hoggs.
The city hall and the police station in the front of it caught fire. The first target of the bombers was a coalition military logistical base. 2 car bombs exploded injuring 15 soldiers. At around the same time another car bomb and mortars were used against a battle group base camp in the city 4-soldiers were killed there and another 15 injured. The 3rd attack targeted a military facility which was on the same side as an Iraqi police station-5 American soldiers were wounded. Other buildings in Kerbala were also hit including city hall which caught fire. A number of Iraqi civilians have been wounded, local hospitals said more than 130 receive treatment. This is the heaviest attack since November when 19 Italian soldiers were killed in Nazaria.

The Head of European Commission Romano Prody narrowly escaped death after a package bomb went off in his hands in his house in Bologna. The bomb was masked as a New

Year's present and and went in flames but failed to explode burning only his carpet and some furniture, Romano Prody said in a TV-interview. A spokesman of the Italian parliament visited Mr. Prodi and confirmed he was unhurt. Both Italian President and Italian prime minister phoned up Mr. Prody to make sure he's alright. Later on Romano Prodi said he'll serve his term to its end. In Afghanistan 2 American soldiers were killed in an ambush of local guerrillas.

< USA-8. TXT >
07 Jan 2004

35 American troops were injured in an attack on an US military base. No further reports came in until it became clear one American and one civilian has died of his wounds later on. Since The USA lanched its war in Iraq on 20th March 2003 a total of 20 British troops and 198 American troops were killed.

08 Jan 2004

An Anerican Blackhawk helicopter was shot down near the volatile Iraqi town of Falluja. 9 people were killed-5 passengers and 4 crew. The helicopter was on a medical r e s q u e mission in medical evacuation mission. 2 Choppers helicopters landed at the crash site while other 2 were hovering above it. Only 6 days earlier another American helicopter was shot down in Iraq-one pilot was killed another injured. An American transport plane came down so the helicopter evacuation mission could be a clear emergency on. Another US plane was shot by an Iraqi missile and was forced to make an emergency landing at Baghdad international air port shortly after its take off. Further details were not reveiled but it is obvious that the huge C-5 cargo jet plane came under flack fire and menaged to return safely after it was hit by a rocket. BBC-Pentagon correspondent Nick Childs said : "Military sources tell us that the C-5 which is a huge plane-about the size of a Jumbo jet-was hit by an anti-air craft rocket while's trying to take off from Baghdad international air port. But it was able to return safely to the air port and there were no injuries among the 63 people on board-52 passengers and 11 crew-the investigation into this case is still continuing but at this stage according to military sources they have reason to believe it was a hostile rocket fire which caused the trouble with this aircraft. The video showed clearly a shoulder fired missile heading up towards the plane and the plane having to return to the Baghdad air port with smoke coming up from one of its engines. At this stage this seems to be scenario ;it is something the US military have been conscience of and trying to take precautions over for a some time. There have been multiple attempts to try to bring an air craft this way around Baghdad international air port and else where. A DHL-freight air craft which appeared to have been hit in a similar way and there was also another reported incident with another US military cargo air plane-a C-17. So this is a contnuing threat which the Americans are having to deal with. This incident is one of just a number that the Americans are having to investigate. At least in this incident were no casualties - unlike many other incidents with US and coalition planes."

The White House stood accused of systematically misrepresenting the threat posed by Saddam Hussein's weapons of mass destruction. The charges were leveled by the US-based think tank-the Karnegie endowment for international peace. It said intelligence officers came under political pressure to make a case for war against Iraq. The Karnegie endowment said it studied hundreds of documents for its report "WMD-evidences and implications". It said there were no convincing evidences Iraq had reconstituted its nuclear program. It sais there was greater uncertainty about biological weapons but that was related to what could be developed in the future. Karnegie sais US officials lumped together Iraqi nuclear, chemical and biological weapons as a single threat despite the different level of danger they posed.

The Pentagon and President George W. Bush were critisized massively by the think tank of Karnegi Endowment for misrepresenting the threat of Iraqi WMD to justify the Iraq war. It became clear Iraq has no WMD and the USA pulled back quitely its 4OO weapon inspectors from Iraq. The Secretary of State Colin Powell said, he had not read the Karnegie-Endowment-report but he also admitted Iraq has no weapons of mass destruction (WMD): BBC_W 19:15 GMT. Later on reporters said : "So far the lie over the Iraq-which had no weapons of mass destruction- came in neither from the British nor from the Americans. Cynicals will be more surprised by the admition not by the lie itself."

4O years ago - in 1964 - President Lindon Johnson declared "unconditional war on poverty and unequality". "This war failed and we have much poverty and unequality even now", said Riccardo Hodgeson in his book "The other America", who's also professor at Columbia University.

Meanwhile it became clear and publically declared the White House report on Weapons of Mass Destruction was exaggerated in order to win public support for the Iraq war. The false information came mostly from the office of the vice-president Dick Chayne but also others falsified reports to make the door open for invasion into Iraq. Now 4OO weapon inspectors left quitely Iraq without reporting any weapons of mass destruction (WMD).

The US Secretary of State Colin Powell who gave a major intelligence presen tation the UN Security Council in February 2OO3 justifying the war against Iraq gave to BBC-World his responce to the Karnegie report: "I have not read the Karnegie report but I'm familiar with it from press accounts this morning. It sais there was capability in Iraq and they were doing this kind of things and they believed that we perhaps overstate them but they don't state WMD weren't there; fact of the matter is Iraq did have weapons of mass destruction in progress, weapons of mass destruction in use-against Iran and against its own people. In 1988 it used them against its own people. Throughout the 198Oies Iraq had every opportunity to comply, to make declarations and get right with the international community, it had the chance to respond to every one of those UNO-resolutions during the 1980ies. When they were threatened by president Clinton in 1998 with bombing and it still didn't comply but forced the inspectors out of the country-this all made a solid case for war to many goverments. This was always a consistent view of UN-inspectors and the US intelligence community that Iraq is a danger we have to warry about".

BBC_World asked Dennis Johnson-associate dean at the graduate school of political menagement at Georgetown University-"What are the political implications of that accusation of systematic mispresentation by the intelligence community and ultimately the White House?" The answer was: "These are pretty harsh words on the part of the Karnegie Institute; the trouble with Secretary Colin Powell's arguments here is that there are a number of people in the US particularly democrates particularly those who're anti-war who will have hard time swallowing this continuing statement that there were no weapons of mass destruction in Iraq and the Karnegie report today is going to add fuel to that fire. It's certainly going to help the presidential frontrunners rather than the Democratic party. Americans are more concerned about the fact that Osama ben Laden is still out there; Americans might be very warried about the number of mounting American casualties we've see even today in the report and this cannot-I think-helpful to the President. The number of continued casualties of American soldiers, brave soldiers abroad is a big problem for the President and the Karnegie report I think certainly does not help the President. The Karnegie report might be completely forgotten to election day but it might become also a major step in the downfall of George Bush."

08 January 2004:

Pakistan started a major attack against al Qaida members in the southern province of Waziristan just accross the border to the Afghani province of Paktika. USA and others have strongly critisized Pakistan for not capable to deal with the insurgency. So long no al Qaida or Taleban fighters were found nor arrested, only local tribal leaders. Paktika has been always a focus of the Afghani anti-American resistence.

2 Afghani soldiers were killed by a bomb explosion in Kandahar while they were on duty. Earlier 2 were killed by another bomb. "President Hamid Karzai is terribly concerned about cross border terrorism. He has good contact with the war lord Ismail Khan and with General Dostum", said Masih Torfe - the human rights adiser of the Afghan president Hamid Karzai in a BBC interview on 08 January 2004.

09 Jan 2004

A bicycle bomb exploded in at the end of Friday prayers in the central Iraqi town of Baquba where at least 9 people were killed and dozens more injured in the blast outside of a packed

Shiite mosque. A gas cylinder filled with explosives and strapped to a bike blew up outside the building;many of those hit were praying on the pavement because of lack of space inside. North of Baghdad Baquba is a largely Suni Muslim area which is a hot bed of resistence to the American led occupation of Iraq. US forces have mounted major operations in and around the town to try to capture those behind the attacks. Targetting Tikrit hundreds of American soldiers have stormed shops and houses in Saddam Hussein's former stronghold in their latest effort to stamp down violence blamed on those loyal to the former leader. Suspects, weapons and other incriminating material were what the troops were looking for and dozens of arrests were made. The army swooped just hours after truck loads of Irakis were released from jail at the start of a wide-ranging prisoner amnesty. The message from the military was clear: there remains no let up in security measures on the ground. "It was a good night", said one senior US officer, adding that Tikrit would be a safer place as a result. The search failed to uncover arms cashes however facked Iraqi police identity cards were among the items found. But as the raids were carried out there was a fresh flair-up of violence elsewhere with rockets fired at a hotel used by Westerners in Baghdad. No one was hurt.

10 January 2004

The International Committee of the Red Cross (ICRC) has renewed a call for the US to grant access to the detained former Iraqi leader Saddam Hussein. The move followed Washington's declaration that Saddam Hussein is officially a prisoner of war. A spokesman for the Red Cross Ion Piper told the BBC that now the Pentagon had clarified his status a visit is essential to asses the conditions of his detention: "We put in our request to visit him as we put in request to visit all those who've been detained in the context of this conflict once we knew they're in the hands of the coalition forces. But clearly the clarification of his status makes it essential that we should see him as soon as possible", said Ion Piper from the Red Cross to the BBC. A member of the American appointed governing council Samir al Sumadai said he hopes that Saddam's PoW status would not limit the amount of information the Americans could get from him. American troops have mistakenly shot dead 2 Iraqi policemen in the town of Kirkuk. A US military spokeswoman said the men were killed when they failed to identify themselves to an US patrol. In December 2003 American troops mistakenly killed 3 Iraqi policemen at a check point in Kirkuk and in September 2003 they killed 10 members of the Iraqi security forces in Falluja.

The Iranian and the Turkish foreign ministers met in Teheran and stressed their will on Iraq's integrity. Any division of Iraq could lead to unacceptable precedent in the region. A French couple of journalists were jailed by a court in Karachi for falling foul of Pakistan's visa regulations. The pair who've admitted visiting a city near the Afghan border without permission have also been fined the equivalent of 1300 euros. Despite the sentence reporter Mark Epstein and photographer Jaean Paul Kiyoto from the French weekly magazin "le Express" were able to walk free from the hearing. The judge has suspended their sentences for a week to give their defence lawyer the chance to appeal. According to news reports they have been working on a documentary about Afghanistan's former Taleban regime to check claims that members of the hard line militia were regrouping in South-Western Pakistan. Their arrest last month drew criticism from international human rights' and media groups.

The US decision to formally declare Saddam Hussein an enemy prisoner of war has caused anger in Iraq. The governing council said it was astonished by the Pentagon's decision which could effect how he is treated in captivity and how he would be trialed. The council insisted the deposed leader must still face an Iraqi court as an Iraqi criminal. But that could clash with Saddam's PoW's status which requires trial by an international tribunal or by the occupying power. Saddam was captured a month earlier in a raid on a farm near his home town of Tikrit.

A demonstration against unemployment in the Southern Iraqi town of Amara turned violent leaving at least 6 protestors dead and several more injured. From the nearby town of Basra the BBC correspondent said, the protest began early in the morning and soon became violent. Angry demonstrators threw stones at Iraqi police and shots were fired. It's still unclear who fired first. Captain Shee Marx from 20th armored brigade sais British troops than moved in with armored vehicles and also came under attack. He said one protester was killed by British forces and another injured. He said the crowd threw explosive devices targetting British soldiers as well as Iraqi police. The crowd of some 500 unemployed men had gathered outside of the city's governor office where the British in whose zone the town lies have their regional headquarters. Eyewitnesses said the Iraqis were protesting about a number of things including the lack of jobs in the region. Eyewitnesses said Iraqi police opened fire killing 4 people after stones were thrown. The demonstrations lasted all day long with sporadic violence.

Captain Marx said British forces came under fire a number of times and had sealed off the area. Coalition forces in Iraq have found a number of mortar rounds that according to initial tests could contain a chemical agent known as blister gas. Danish soldiers found 36 of the shells on the day before-Friday-North of Basra where British troops are located too. The Danish army said the weapons have been burried for at least 10 years. The Iraqis used blister gas during the war against Iran from 1980 to 1988.

A bomb explosion in a crowded cafe in the Indonesian town of Polopo in South Suluwazi province has killed 4 people;several other people were injured and taken to hospital. Polopo is some 300km South of the Pousso region in Central Suluwazi where clashes between Muslims and Christians increased towards the end of 2003 despite the signing of a peace deal in 2001. Peter Miles-the BBC correspondent in Indonesia-said the bomb exploded in a crawded cafe late in the evening. A local police official told the BBC that the device was planted under the table and the victims were all local people. There was no indication so far as to who might planted the bomb and why. The police spokesman said he was surprised of the blast as the area was generally peaceful. Any recent violence in South Sulawazi has been between villagers over local issues - such as land disputes. A more serious conflict has been continuing about 300km North in Central Suluwazi between Christians and Muslims. The last similar incident in South Suluwazi was a bomb attack on a McDonald restaurant in the city of Makassa at the end of 2002. Several Islamic militants jailed for that attack were suspected of having links with the bombers of a night club in Balli earlier in 2002.

11 January 2004

7 Iraqi men were arrested and a big cash of weapons uncovered by the Americans in the town of Baquba. A woman threw a grenade at them but it failed to explode. The British prime minister Tony Blair expressed doubt if weapon of mass destruction ever could be found in Iraq.

12 January 2004

American troops shot dead 7 Iraqis when they were steeling oil from a pipe line. An American spokesman there was a g u n f i g h t at the scene near the town of Samara North of Baghdad where American forces tried to make arrests. Fuel pipe lines are popular targets for insurgents who oppose the American occupation as well for common criminals After a tip off from a local villager the Americans surrounded the oil thieves and opened fire. In Ramadi skirmishes took place in a fire exchange. One Iraqi and one captain were killed. His nationality was not disclosed.

****

The US treasure department has ordered an investigation into whether a critic of President George W. Bush-the former treasury secretary Paul O'Neil improperly disclosed one or more secrete documents to a TV-program. Paul O'Neil who's contributed to a new book on the Bush administration has alleged that George Bush intended to oust Saddam Hussein even before the 11ᵗʰ September attacks 2001. The Washington BBC-correspondent Justine Webb reported, President Bush stands accused by his former treasury secretary Paul O'Neil of looking for an excuse from the very moment he arrived in the White House to attack Saddam Hussein. In interview to publicize a book Paul O'Neil has added that he as member of the President's National Security Team never saw any evidence that weapons of mass destruction exist in Iraq. In response the President said that as previous US administrations he had been for a regime change but he suggested that the task only became urgent after the terrorist attacks on America in 2001. Within the administration there's a wide spread annoyance of Paul O'Neil's comments and his decision to show documents he said were secret in a TV-program publisizing his book has led the treasury department investigation to see whether its former boss Paul O'Neil has broken any law (and certainly it will). Paul O'Neil was accused initially of steeling 1, OOOs of documents and revealing them to a TV-program.

He accused President Bush of making the war against Iraqi people his priority already on the 10th day of his arriving to the White House-well 12 months in advance of the 11ᵗʰ September attacks on New York and Washington. The book re-echoed what many democrates and many ordinary people in USA already believed-president George W. Bush were disengaged and manipulated. One of these secret documents revealed in O'Neil's book is that president Bush planed access to Iraqi oil wells in case of eventual war on Iraq. Now it has been check whether Paul O'Neil is in breach with US state secrecy laws.

Visiting by that time Mexico on a summit of 30 American nations President Bush said: "I appreciate highly the service of Paul O'Neil to our country" but silencing the fact he fired Paul O'Neil from the Treasury Department 10 months earlier. George Bush disfigured clearly his face into a malicious grimace when asked this quastion in a TV-interview on 12 January 2004. Paul O'Neil said: "I've never seen any weapons of mass destruction (WMD) in the papers and the papers were not secret; the whole Iraq-war was unjustified and premeditated!" This scandal will develop further.

6 people have appeared before anti-terrorism judges in France accused of providing assistence to a group ploting to plant a chemical atack. The 6-who include 2 Muslim imams- Jelali ben Jelali and Murad Murabet- are from the Lyon area and were arrested the week before. They're placed under former investigation by magistrates. Their arrest came as a part of long running French intelligence operation looking for links between French Islamic extremists and rebels in Chechnya.

13 January 2004

An American military helicopter has come down in an area West of Baghdad. The US military confirmed the incident but have given no details and it is not known if there are any casualties. The helicopter came down near the town of Habaniya- an area known for attacks by guerrillas on US forces. A Soviet-built air craft YAK-40 crashed in Uzbekistan shortly before landing at Dushanbe air port. All 37 people on board were killed including the UN official Richard Konnoy.

The plane crashed in thick fog after circling twice over the airport but in landing the landing device failed to engage and the plane hit a fence near the airport, Uzbeck officials said excluding any terrorist attack.

14 January 2004 Wendsday:

The Supreme Court in Afghanistan has complained to the goverment after state television broadcast footage of an Afghan woman singing for the first time in more than a decade. The deputy chief Justice Feisel Ahmed Manawoui said the Court was opposed to women singing and dancing and the broad cast defy the constitution and previous Court decisions. He said it would be up to the Goverment to decide what action to take if any;the broad cast contained archive footage of Sirma-a star of the 1970ies and 80ies-singing a romantic ballade: (Sirma in translation means "Silk"" or silk-textile with golden or silver fibres within).

US military announced the arrest of a cleric who was on its list of its most wanted Iraqis. Brigadier General Mark Kemmit said Hamiz Sa(r)han al Mohamed-the local Baath leader in the town of Falluja under Saddam Hussein have been arrested in Ramadi West of Baghdad on Sunday 11-01-2004-and today we have 14-01-2004 Wendsday: the US spokesman described him as an enabler for many of the attacks have been carried out on American forces: "With the capture of NR.54 we've taken another signifficant step into reducing anti-coalition resistence; he was an enable of many of the resistence attacks on Iraqis (who were earlier brought to starvation by US and UN measures, resolutions and embargoes) as well as US and coalition forces. His attacks were crimes against the Iraqi people. The coalition in an inner circle (staggering and stottering these words); and governing council had the resolve (or ressources?) to see this process through to the end (... and what is the end??) ... Former regime owners that support and condoled violence The Hardest and terrorist have no place in a free and democratic Iraq.", said US Brigadier General Mark Kemmit (spelled also otherwise) to the media.

*

The US Secretary of State Colin Powell justifued the American agression on Iraq saying that Iraq still has hidden weapons of mass destruction which only wait for the Americans to find them. The US troops toppled the regime of Saddam Hussein in April 2003 but since than no weapons of mass destruction were found - neither by Americans nor by Brits.

*

A court in Spain have sentenced a man because of his book "How to beat their wives without leaving incriminating marks. The cleric Mohamed Kemal Mustafa will not have to serve time in jail because Spanish law automatically suspends sentences of less than 2 years for first offences. Mr. Mustafa's book out raged women's groups when it was published in 2001.

14 January 2004 Wendsday: Virgine-an US Airways-allowing a Sudanese born passenger to board their plane from Washington to London with life ammunition in his pockets on 14-01-2004;he was arrested upon his arrival in Heathrow airport:the case was particularly embarassing for the USA giving the recent pressure they've been exerting on other countries to do more to protect commercial aviation. The US goverment said it is working with the Virgine airways and law-enforcement agencies both in the USA and in Britain. An officicial of Transportation Security Administration told the BBC that an investigation was underway. The TSA was looking at the records at Dallas airport but so far the search had not been completed. How some one can board a plane at Dallas to London carrying live ammunition is a mistery. Security at the airport is particularly tight with extensive checks performed on passengers and their hand luggage before they're allowed anywhere near the boarding areas. That such a laps occured is particularly embarrassing for the US authorities given the recent pressure they've been exerting on other countries to do more to protect commercial daviation.

*

The American Secretary of State Colin Powell has again defended the decision to attack Iraq insisting that there was still reason to believe Iraq has weapon of mass destructions and that the search for them is not over yet. He told the BBC that the US went to war because "Iraq was run by a dangerous regime". He said that the failure to find weapons of mass destruction did not mean that intelligence reports have been based on faulty assumptions.

*

In Washington former American Treseary Secretary Paul O'Neil was accused of releasing secrete documents to the public in a TV-talk show. In his book on Bush's administration he put it that President George W. Bush was intending to unleash a war on Iraq far earlier than 11th September attacks. As for me I remember clearly the war on Iraq was stated clearly as a major goal in Bush's pre-eletion agenda in 2000.

As BBC-correspondent in Washington Mark Frey and Bob Landsey-former advisor to George W. Bush-put it: for the Bush's opposers this will be a vindication but his supporters will rally support behind the President. The campaign may develop as Monika Lewinsky sleaze did-is my personal opinion.

*

There have been 2 explosion near a military base in the southern Afghan city Kandahar. The latest reports said 12 people died and 46 were injured including many women and children when the device attached to a bicycle went off. Afghan and American forces have sealed off the area where the blast occured. Guerrillas loyal to the former Taleban authority have been blamed for a sery of attacks and kidnappings in Southern Afghanistan centered around the former Taleban stronghold of Kandahar. The explosion underlined the ongoing instability in the region just 2 days after the Grand Council-the Loya Jirgaof tribal leaders-aproved the charters supposed to pin a new more powerful independant state. Kandehar is a former stronghold of the Taleban and Afghan officials have described the explosion as a terrorist attack. However a spokesman for members of the ousted regime reportedly denied any involvement.

*

15-01-2004 Thursday

The top UN official for Afghanistan-Lakhdar Brahimi - has warned that without greater security and stronger governors the Afghan reconstruction will be at risc. In a final briefing before leaving office he told the UN Security Council that what have been achieved in Afghanistan so far had to be built on quickly. Police in Pakistan said at least 11 people were injured in a bomb attack on a church in the southern church in Karachi. Police officials said the attackers threw fire crackers at a bible society and a Christian library belonging to one of the city's churches;when people started coming out to see what's had happened a car bomb exploded causing the injuries. The assailants are believed to have escaped. There was a spate of attacks against Christians in Pakistan in 2002.

*

One of the most senior Shiite clerics in Iraq has written a strongly worded letter to President Bush and the British prime minister Tony Blair quastioning their sincerity in wanting to transfer power to the Iraqis. In his letter he said the current plan for political transition had not to do with the American presidential election and Iraqi interests;and he warned the consequences of ignoring Iraqi demands. The letter came as tens of thousands Iraqis demonstrated in the southern city of Basra against the plan agreed between the US and the Iraqi Governing Council (council in translation means Soviet). Mac de Altrahadia BBC Arab speaking journalist in Iraq reported:Hodja al Islam Ali Abdul Hakim al Sofi accused the American-led coalition of insencerity:he said the coalition argument about the logistical difficulties involved in organizing elections is simply a pretext to deny the Iraqis their legitimate aspiration: "Lack of an up to date censeses should not be an unsurmountable obstacle and election based on an all census is far better than no election at all. The letter concludes with a vague warning to President Bush and to Tony Blair: "You will drag your countries into a battle that you'll lose if you do not let the Iraqis choose their own institutions"", he said: "The current plan for political transition had more to do with American presidential election than with Iraqi interests."

His letter came as 1Os of thousands of Iraqis demonstrated in the southern city of Basra calling for direct election of a new goverment - not indirect selection as proposed by the US. Tens of thousands Iraqis have been demostrating at the main Shiite mosque in the southern city of Basra to demand direct election to Iraq's new administration. Speaker after speaker called for the rejection of the American proposal that the new authority be selected rather than elected. BBC correspondent Dimitra Luhtra was at the rally: "It was a show of power, a show of influence. Tens of thousands of Shiite came to Ayatollah Said Ali Hakim-a stream pastor's mosque in Basra. He called them out to show the Americans the strength of Shiites in Iraq and he succeeded;he told them to demonstrate peacefully-again he succeeded. It sends a clear message to the Americans: "We can mobilize the people against you if we need to". The rally was called after the top Shiite in Iraq - Grand Ayatollah Ali Sustany - rejected the US plan for transitional goverment in the country. He said, the National Assembley which is to choose the goverment must be elected not selected as is the current plan.

Iraqi banknotes bearing the face of Saddam Hussein seize to be legal tendar today. New notes carrying pictures of historic Iraqi sites have been in circulation for the past 3 months and their value's risen sharply as currency dealers anticipate a surge of American money into the country to finance reconstruction projects.

*

The South Korean foreign minister Yion Young Yayh-resigned upon the issue of American military bases on Korean soil. A member of an unofficial US-delegation visited North Korea's nuclear complex has said the North-Koreans have told the group that spent nuclear fuel rods have been reprocessed to extract plutonium-the material used in A-bombs. Charles Prichard-a former State Department official-said there is no way of independantly verifying the claim. Prichard said that he was shown the empty canisters that once held the rods until all 8OOO rods had been reprocessed to extract the plutonium-the material used in nuclear bombs. BBC journalist in Washington Jannet Jallil explained: "Charles Prichard confirmed that the delegation have been shown around the nuclear facility in Young Byang-the first time outsiders've been allowed in since North Korea reactivated its nuclear plant there and expelled UN-inspectors just over a year earlier. The delegation's visit was a private one-not sanctioned by the American goverment - but Charles Prichard said the aim was to help bring about another round of talks between the USA, North Korea and 4 of its neighbours possibly by February 2OO4.

16 January 2004

The American administrator in Iraq Paul Bremer met in Washington President George W. Bush to discuss mounting tensions over plans to hand over the power to Iraqis by June 2004. Strong opposition from the spiritual leader of Iraq's Shiite majority has jeopardized White House proposals for regional meetings to select their transitional authority. The cleric Ali Asustani has demanded direct elections. One of his aids has warned that Shiite leaders may issue a ruling banning Shiites from supporting the US-lead authorities in Iraq. "Paul Bremer is in Washington because the US plan to transfer power to Iraqis is in trouble. Iraq's most revered Shiite cleric Ayatolah Ali al Sustani is refusing to support it. He said, he wants an elected Iraqi goverment not a selected one. If the Americans ignore him they risc seeing the legitimacy of their plans undermined. This could increase political tensions in Iraq. The Bush administration has an extra reason for wanting the hand-over in June to go smoothly - the US Presidential election which is due to be held a few months later-in November 2004. On Monday-19 January 2004 Paul Bremer will go to New York to meet UN Secretary General Kofi Annan to see if can persuade the UN to help the Americans hand over power to the Iraqis", said the BBC correspondent in Washington Janet Jalil.

*

The White House said it is willing to amend its plans for handing over power in Iraq in the face of opposition from the country's majority Shiite community. The senior US administrator in Iraq Paul Bremer is meeting President Bush in Washington now to discuss how to respond to the demand for direct elections made by the Shiite spiritual leader Ayatollah Ali al Sustani. From Washington BBC-correspondent Justin Webb said: "The Grand Ayatollah is regarded as moderate so when his supporters talk of more protests, a general strike and possibility of religious edict undermining the authority of America's plans for the hand-over of power the White House is bound to listen and listen hard. Mr. Bremer needs to know how flexible the President and his advisors are prepared to be. Official said the President is willing to refine or improve his plans for regional meetings to choose members of the new Iraqi Parliament perhaps providing more direct voter participation but it is not clear whether he's considering the kind of open elections which might satisfy the Shiites but take more time to set up".

Turkey's powerful military has warned that the establishment of federation in Iraq could lead to difficult and bloody future for the country especially if it would be based on ethnic ground. The Turkish deputy Chief of Staff Ilke Bashpu said: "If the Iraqi people did vote for a federal system of goverment after the Americans hand over power than it will be better to do this on geographical lines". The BBC-correspondent in Istambul Johnnie Diamand considers: "Senior officers of the Turkish army do not normally give news conferences. Their influence - not as great as it was – but still formidable in matters of national security is generally felt in more discrete ways. But General Bashpu has spelt out the military's view of the ongoing debate about Iraq's eventual structure. It mirrors that of Turkish goverment and Turkey's neighbours Iran and Syria. All 3 of Iraq's Northern neighbours oppose an autonomous Kurdish region in the North of Iraq. All 3 fear that such a region would destabilize their own Kurdish populations.

*

An advanced contingent of Japanese soldiers has left for Iraq in what is Japan's first deployment of troops into a conflict area since the second world war.

At a solemn military ceremony to mark their departure the Japanese defence minister Shigero Oshiba said "their task is noble one":Japan is to send a 600 strong force to Southern Iraq in February 2004 to help the US-led coalition. Their role will be strictly humanitarian but they will still be armed and critics say this violates Japan's pacifist constitution.

17 January 2004:

A bomb attack on an American armoured vehicle north of the Iraqi Capital Baghdad have killed 3 US soldiers and 2 members of the Iraqi civil defence forces;2 other American soldiers on a joint patrol were injured in the incident in the town of Taji-some 30 km from the Capital. The US military said the joint American-Iraqi patrol was doing a sweep for road side bombs when it struck one. The heavily armoured Bradley-fighter vehicle leading the patrol caught fire and was destroyed. But American officials say generally attacks are decreasing and Britains top soldier - General Sir Michael Jackson agrees : "The evidence is that the level of violence has decreased quite signifficantly right across Iraq;in the South in the British area in and around Basra it has been always a lesser problem any way ", he said to the BBC-correspondent Barbara Plett: "The coalition's concern is to get from where we're now within an improving situation through complicated 5 months to the transfer of authority on 1st of July and keep the various pieces of it match together;so it is successful". With this attack the number of the American soldiers killed in Iraq after the end of the war in March 2003 rose to 500. American military official said the US is preparing to cut the number of its troops in Iraq by 25,000. A US Army spokesman told reporters in a briefing that American military command had decided to reduce the US presence from its current level of around 140,000 to about 105,000. One report quotes him saying the number of tanks will be cut by 75%, the number of helicopters-by nearly 40% and the artillery and rockets deployed will also substantially scaled back.

*

The Afghan Supreme Court has expressed its anger of TV-broadcast which was showing an Afghan woman singer performing during its evening broadcast. The transmission came despite a demand by the Supreme Court that such broad casts be banned as un-Islamic. The raw began when Kabul state television first showed the woman singing earlier that week breaking a tabu which dates back to fall of the Communist goverment 12 years earlier. The minister for women's affairs Habiba Surabi told the BBC that men and women had equal rights and the broadcast had the support of the people.

*

18 January 2004

A 500 kilo car-bomb has exploded outside the main headquarters of the US-led coalition in Baghdad killing at least 20 people. Most of the victims were Iraqis who work inside the complex. They were queueing up (on Sunday??) waiting to be searched when the bomb went off aparantly detonated by the driver. Coalition officials told a news conference they believed it was a suicide attack and at least 2 Americans were among the dead. More than 60 other people were injured.

It is the deadliest single attack since the former Iraqi leader Saddam Hussein was captured in mid December 2003. The BBC correspondent in Baghdad Alastar Lieshead said: "A line of body bags lies beside the burnt-out wreckage of vehicles that were passing the coalition headquarters at O8:OO in the morning when a suicide bomber struck. 500 kg of explosives are estimated to have been packed into a white pick-up truck and detonated outside the checkpoint on the edge of the security area known as "the Green Zone". Dozens of Iraqi people working for the coalition were queueing up waiting to be searched. A spokesman for the Iraqi governing council Hamid Al Kafai condemned the attack: "It was hideous attack happening at a time when thousands of Iraqis were preparing to leave for the Haji-pilgrimage for the first time in 25 years; this despicable act of terrorism will not deter us from moving forward and building a stable, democratic and free Iraq", he said in English.

*

There's been another explosion in the northern Iraqi city of Tikrit where a bomb went off inside a car killing 2 Iraqis. Another Iraqi man in the vehicle was seriously injured. The Americans said it apeared that the man have been planing to attack a US patrol but their bomb had gone off prematurely. One reports said, one of the men killed was a relative of the former Iraqi leader Saddam Hussein. A military spokesman said the car-a white Mercedes-was believed to have been used in previous attacks against the US-led coalition forces.

*

The authorities in Pakistan said they have arrested 7 people suspected of having links with the Al Qaida network. The 5 men and 2 women were detained in raids in the port city of Karachi; they are said to be foreign nationals. Pistols and hand grenades were seized during the raids that led to the arrest. Since the attacks on the US in September 2001 Pakistan has arrested dozens of suspected Al Qaida members and handed them over to the American authorities.

****

18 January 2004

Supporters of the jailed former deputy prime minister of Malaysia Anwar Ibrahim said they're going ahead with a protest rally despite the police ban. The demonstration due to be held near the Capital Kuala Lumpur is part of the 4-week campaign aimed at achieving Mr. Anwar's release. He's dismissed in 1998 by the than Prime Minister Dr. Mohatir Mohamed and is currently serving 15 years in jail on corruption and sex charges. Jonnatan Kent-BBC correspondent in Malaysia said from Kuala Lumpur "with an election on the horizon Malaysia's political opposition intends to find out whether the new prime minister is true to his word. When he took power in November 2003 Abdula Badawi promised he'd accept criticism and contrary views. But the organizers of the Sunday's rally said they're refused permition to their meeting on grounds of internal security despite having been given a permit days before. However earlier this weekend 2 motorcades in support of Mr. Anwar were allowed to drive around the country with minimum interference from the authorities."

18 January 2004

King Noradon Sianuk of Cambodia has expressed sadness over the adoption of Cambodian babies by foreigners. King Sianuk said extreme poverty had pushed some parents into selling their children to people from wealthier nations.

26 January 2004 Monday

The President of Afghanistan's transitional goverment Hamid Karzai has signed the country's new constitution 3 weeks after it was aproved by the Grand Assembly or Loya Jirga. The signing ceremony in Kabul was attended by Afghan goverment ministers and ambassadors from around the world. The constitution invisages a strong Presidency and enshrines eqaul rights for men and women. During the signing ceremony in the Afghani foreign ministry marble hall Hamid Karzai was given a golden pen by the Afghan King Zahir Shah to sign with, as shown on BBC-screen.

****

****

Subgatullah Mujadhidin-Chairman of the Afghani Grand Assembly Loya Jirga in January 2004 Celestine Perissinotto-spokeswoman for the Swiss Federal Office for Civil Aviation;on TV on 04-01-2004

Sharm el-Sheikh-Egyptian Red Sea resort where a plane crashed on 03-01-2004 killing 148 people on board.

Sheikh Rashid-Pakistani information minister

Khumadoud Udsai-President's Karzai's Chief of staff

Noratula-province of South-Eastern Thailand where many terrorist attacks took place in January 2004

Acceh-separatist province in Indonesia

Sultana-residential district in the Saudi capital Riyadh where a bomb was found on05 Jan 2004

Kuala Tiringanu-Malaysian city

Jilbert de Robienne-French transportation minister on the Flash Airlines

Aguino Mousselier-French minister visited the site of the air crash in Sharm el-Sheikh on 04-01-2004

Gerd Potter-German MEP, to whom a parcell-bomb was sent on 05 January 2004

Gary Titley-British MEP, to whom a parcell-bomb was sent on 05 January 2004

Patani-province in Southern Thailand, where a bomb went off on 05 January 2004

Noratula-province in South-Eastern Thailand, where a bomb went off on 04 January 2004

****

Jaean Paul Kiyoto-photographer from the French weekly magazine "le Express", arrested in Pakistan in December 2003, sentenced to 6 months jail and 1300 eur fine

Mark Epstein-reporter from the French weekly magazin "le Express", arrested in Pakistan in December 2003, sentenced to 6 months jail and 1300 eur fine

****

the atmosphere was infused with citronic smell
kewed
a spin around
sand shoes army
sand shoes camp

Masih Torfe - HR-adiser of the Afghan president Hamid Karzai;gave BBC interview on 08 January 2004

Waziristan - province in Pakistan, just across the Afghan province of Paktika where Pakistani troops launched a major attack against al Qaida and Taleban troops on 08 January 2004

Heba Saleh-BBC Cairo

Paktika - provinve in Afghanistan

Riccardo Hodgeson - author of a book on American poverty "The other America", professor at the Columbia University. BBC-interview on 08 January 2004

Bangalore - India's own Silicon Valley

Balad - Iraqi city South-West from Baghdad where road side bomb killed 4 American soldiers on 04-01-2004

Loyal Jerga >> Loya Jirga

Faisal Saleh Hayat - Pakistany foreign minister

Sanjeev Srivastava - BBC correspondent in Islamabad

Lee Jung Hoon - BBC correspondent in Seoul; professor

Yasakuna shrine - a military temple in Japan, visited on 08-01-2004 by the Japanese prime minister Junisicho Kuizumi among international criticism

Sibgatullah Mujahedeen - Chairman of the Loya Jirga

Francesc Vendrell - EU-representative at the Loya Jirga, critisized the Jirga as undemocratic on 04-01-2004 in BBC_W at 16:14, in 2001/02 he was a special UN-envoy to Afghanistan

George Perkovic - from Karnegi endowment, interviewed by BBC on 08-01-2004 at 19:00 GMT critisized America's war on Iraq

Ken Adelman - from Pentagon defence board, interviewed by BBC on 08-01-2004 at 19:00 GMT

Dennis Johnson - associate dean at the graduate school of political menagement at Georgetown university, critic of the US-war on Iraq on 08-01-2004 in BBC_W 19:10 GMT

Shazia Miars - British Muslim woman comedian 21, critisized America and its Iraq war but "Americans didn't laugh because they're afraid of Muslim women and they didn't know whether they're allowed to laugh or not", BBC_W interview on 08-01-2004 19:18 GMT

Medameggi Melay - British entertainer, ridiculed the war on 08-o1-2004 in BBC at 19:15 GMT

Halid al Awwadi - Saudi education minister, interviewed in BBC_W on 08-01-2004 at 19:14 GMT

Paktika - Afghani province just accros of the Pakistani Weziristan; has been always a focus of the Afghani anti-American resistence.

Riccardo Hodgeson - Professor at Columbia University, author of the book "The other America", which is on American poverty home

****

just nudging -?
local scorners
a brain storm
lump together
lui = lazy

****

blister gas-chemical poisonous gas used by Saddam Hussein in the war against Iran 1980-1988

Captain Shee Marx - commander of British 20th armoured division in Basra, Southern Iraq

Peter Miles - BBC correspondent in Indonesia in 2004

Alastar Mope-BBC correspondent in Basra, South Iraq

Peter Miles - BBC correspondent Indonesia in 2004

Matt Frei - BBC correspondent in Washington

Polopo- Indonesian town in South Suluwasy province where bomb exploded on 10-01-2004 killing 4 people;it'sconnected with the bombers of Balli in Indonesia in 2002

South Suluwazi - Indonesian province

Suluwazi - Indonesian province with clashes between Muslims and Christians despite the signing of a peace deal in 2001

Makassa - town in Suluwazi in Indonesia where a McDonald restaurant was blown up end of 2002

Tikrit - home town of Iraqi dictator Saddam Hussein where he was finally arrested on 13 December 2003

Pousso-Indonesian region in Central Suluwazi with clashes between Muslims and Christians in 2003-04

Damny Fillister- BBC correspondent in Basra, Iraq in 2004

John Lewis - American weapon inspector, visited the North Korean nuclear complex on 09 Jan 2004:

"North Korean officials honoured all US requests. Declined to give details because he "must first brief the US goverment".

Koreans and Americans were shown what is termed "North Korean nuclear deterrent force at Yongbyon" but he didn't explane what this meant.

Waziristan - southern Pakistani province just accross the border to the Afghan province of Paktika;Pakistanis launched a massive attack on Taleban on 08-01-2004

Haward Dean - US Democratic party activist, critisized by Professor Dennis Johnson in BBc-interview on 09-01-2004

Ion Piper - spokesman for the Red Cross

Samir al Sumadai - member of the American appointed governing council in Iraq

Thaksim Shinowatra-Thai prime minister, in 2004 imposed marshal law in 3 Southern mainly Muslim Thai provinces; promised to bring prosperity to them;acknowledged wide-spread goverment corruption

James Muir - BBC-corresponder in Teheran

Abadan - Iranian oil city

O'Neil - American jpurnalist critical on Bush administration. In his book he revealed George W. Bush intended to unleash war on Iraqi people earlier than 11th Semptember-this was indeed his preelection campaign.

Larry Lindsay-former advisor of President Bush

Samara - Iraqi town North of Baghdad where American forces tried to make arrests on 12 January 2004. They shot dead 7 Iraqis who were obviously not armed.

Paul O'Neil - US Treasury department secretary; critical on G.W. Bush war against Iraqi people in an exposing book on the Bush administration. Fired by G.W. Bush in May 2003. On TV-interviews on 12 January 2004 was very critical

Jelali ben Jelali - Muslim imam arrested in Lyon in France on 12 Jan 2004 for connection with Islamic terrorists and Chechnya rebels.

Murad Murabet-Muslim imam arrested in Lyon in France on 12 Jan 2004 for connection with Islamic terrorists and Chechnya rebels.

Habaniya- town West of Baghdad known for guerrilla-attacks on US forces;US military helicopter was shot down there on 13-01-2004.

Marinesku - U-boot commander of T13, who sank the German ship Gustloff in 1945
Pommernland is abgebrannt
Gau - province, district
Ubergriff - zlodejanie
www. zdf. de
www.sternenfluestern.zdf. de
www.daserste. de
CDC - onderzoek institute in Lelystad
Mit wenig Geld auskommen = mit wenig Geld wirtschaften
Karl Lagerfeld - in ZDF with sheer dark glasses on 13-01-2004
Richard Konnoy- UN official died in a plane crash in Uzbekistan on 13-10-2004
Martin Markow-Marccello

Habaniya- town and area known for attacks by guerrillas on US forces. A US military helicopter came down there shot by Iraqi guerrillas on 14-01-2004

Feisel Ahmed Manawoui-Iraqi Deputy chief of Justice, made assessment of the situation on 14-01-2004 after an US military helicopter was shot down by guerrillas in Baquba area.

Mark Kemmit - US Brigadier General in Iraq who arrested the local Baath leader Hamiz Sahan al Mohamed on 14-01-2004 in the town of Falluja

Hamiz Sahan al Mohamed- the local Baath leader in the town of Falluja, arrested by US Brigadier General Mark Kemmit on 14-01-2004: NR.54 on the American most wanted list

Hamiz Sarhan al Mohamed- the local Baath leader in the town of Falluja, arrested by US Brigadier General Mark Kemmit on 14-01-2004: NR.54 on the American most wanted list

Ramadi- Iraqi city West to Baghdad where on Sunday 11-01-2004 Baath activists were arrested

Mohamed Kemal Mustafa - Spanish author of the book "How to beat wives without leaving incriminating remarks", published in 2001

Virgine- US Airways allowing a Sudanese born passenger to board their plane from Washington to London with life ammunition in his pockets on 14-01-2004; he was arrested upon his arrival in Heathrow airport: the case was particularly embarassing for the USA giving the recent pressure they've been exorting on other countries to do more to protect commercial aviation. The US goverment said it is working with the Virgine airways and law-enforcement agencies both in the USA and in Britain. An officicial of transportation security administration told the BBC that an investigation was underway. The TSA was looking at the record at Dallas airport but so far the search had not been completed. How some one can board a plane at Dallas to London carrying live ammunition is a mistery. Security at the airport is particularly tight with extensive checks performed on passengers and their hand luggage before they're allowed anywhere near the boarding areas. That such a laps occured is particularly embarrassing for the US authorities given the recent pressure they've been exorting on other vountries to do more to protect commercial aviation.

Yion Young Yayh-korean foreign minister resigned upon the issue of American military bases in South Korea on 15 January 2004

Jakob Killenberger - President of the ICRC, visited USA on 15 January 2004 incuding the military Guantanamo jail in Cuba

Charles Prichard - former State Department official, visited on 15-01-2004 the North Korean nuclear reactor at Yong Byong-said the North-Koreans have told the group that spent nuclear fuel roads have been reprocessed to extract plutonium-the material used in A-bombs. Charles Prichard said there is no way of independantly verifying the claim.

Basra - city in southern Iraq occupied by British troops; the northern part of Iraq was occupied by Americans. Iraqi Governing Council - provisional puppet body appointed by the US to govern Iraq transitionally; but from the fall of Saddam Hussein in April 2003 till April 2004 a whole year elapsed without any sustaintial changes

Mac de Altrahadi - a BBC Arab speaking journalist in Iraq reported on tummults and anti-American and anti-British demonstrations in Iraq in winter of 2004

Hodja al Islam Ali Abdul Hakim al Sofi - senior Shiite cleric in Iraq, on 15-01-2004 wrote an open letter to Tony Blair and George W. Bush accusing them publicly in manipulation

Jannet Jallil - BBC journalist in Washington, on 15-01-2004 elucidated on North Korean nuclear reprocessing

Young Byang - North Korean nuclear facility shown to an US delegation on 15-01-2004

Dimitra Luhtra - BBC correspondent in Iraq

Ayatollah Said Ali Hakim-senior Shiite in Basra who set out the people against the American occupation in 2004 (15 January 2004)

Grand Ayatollah Ali Sustany - top Shiite in Iraq

Habiba Surabi-Afghani minister for women's affairs in 2004

Taji - Iraqi town some 30 km from the Capital Baghdad, where Iraqi guerrillas attacked an US armoured vehicle and kille 3 US soldiers in a bomb attack on 17-01-2004

Barbara Plett - BBC correspondent in Iraq in 2004

Bradley - heavily armoured US vehicle

Sir Michael Jackson - British General, top commander in Iraq

Ali Asustani - Ayatolah, Iraq's supreme Shiite spiritual leader opposed to American plans for selected MPs;he demanded direct elections warned that Shiite leaders may issue a ruling banning Shiites from supporting the US-lead authorities in Iraq. Generally he's regarded as moderate.

Janet Jalil - BBC correspondent in Washington in 2004

Shigero Oshiba - Japanese defence minister, in January 2004 dispatched Japanese troops to Iraq

Ilke Bashpu - Turkish deputy chief of staff in 2004

Abdulah Badawi - Malaysian President

Jack Straw - British dfence minister under Tony Blair; under John Major was interior minister

Sirma- Afghan star of the 1970ies and 80ies;many performed many talk- and singing shows

Robert Killroy Silk - a British TV-moderator;after insulting remarks to Arabs was forced to step down in January 2004

Alastar Lieshead - BBC correspondent in Baghdad in 2004

Green Zone - the security area in Baghdad after the fall of Saddam Hussein

Hamid Al Kafai - spokesman for the Iraqi governing council in 2004

Anwar Ibrahim - former deputy prime minister of Malaysia, now in jail for 15 years for corruption

Mohatir Mohamed - prime minister of Malaysia for 21 years;in November 2003 resigned voluntarily from his post. Doctor of Law, accused falsely his deputy Anwar Ibrahim and put him to jail in 1998 for 15 years.

Jonnatan Kent - BBC correspondent in Malaysia

Abdula Badawi - Malaysian prime minister from November 2003

motorcade - procession of motor bikes

Noradon Sianuk - King of Cambodia

Sianainn - (= Shanan) = Irish airfield where an American plane owned by Delta-airlines on its way from Frankfurt to Atlanta was forced to emergency landing on a false bomb alarm on 18-01-2004.

< USA-9. TXT >

19 January 2004 Monday

Afghan officials said 11 people have been killed in an American attack on a village in Uruzgan province north of Kandahar;the provincial governor Jam Mohamed Khan told the BBC the US-aircraft attacked on Saturday night and more than half the dead were women or children. BBC correspondent in Kabul Andrew North said, "local officials said the Afghans died after a US strike on a village in the Char-Chino district of Uruzgan province in the early hours of Sunday (18 January 2004). It is an area where US troops regularly clash with suspected Taleban fighters. But as always with such incidents there are conflicting accounts of what happened. The provincial governor said, all of those killed were civilians and said the village have been searched by US soldiers the day before. An American military spokesman lt. colonnel Brian Healtherty confirmed to the BBC an air strike in the same part of Uruzgan province on Sunday 18 January 2OO4. 5 people were killed, he said, people he described as members of an armed anti-coalition militia".

*

19 January 2004 Monday

The UN Secretary General Kofi Annan said, he's received a request from the US and the American appointed Iraqi governing council to send a team to Baghdad to assess whether elections can held by May 2OO4. After meeting the American administrator for Iraq Paul Bremer and the Iraqi leaders Mr. Annan said the decision on any UN involvement would only be made after further discussions on technical details. Paul Bremer said, an agreement has been reached during their meeting.

Earlier in Baghdad ten of thousands of Shiites demonstrated in support of their call for elections. A spokesman for their most senior cleric Ayatollah Sistani said he might reconsider his position if an independent UN team decided it is not yet feasible to hold elections.

A former employee of a British intelligence agency is to go on a trial next month for informing a newspaper that the US asked the agency to spy on members of the UN Security Council ahead of the war in Iraq. The former employee-Catrine Gun-worked at the British Intelligence Gathering Center JCHQ. She doesn't deny leaking a confidential memo in which American official asks British agents to listen out for information that might help the US win a Security Council vote on Iraq.

*

2O January 2004 Tuesday A big demonstration took place in the Iraqi Capital Baghdad. The rally came as UN Secretary General Kofi Annan was considering sending a team to assess whether direct elections can be held in Iraq within the next few months. Thousands of Shiite suporters of the radical cleric Mokhtada Asadar marched through Baghdad to condemn any move to turn Iraq into a federal state. He also joint the calls for immediate direct elections. The BBC correspondent in Baghdad Barbara Plett said, this was a much smaller demonstration compared with the demonstration the day before called by the Grand Ayatollah Ali al Sistani-the most popular and powerful Shiite cleric in Iraq. This demonstration was called by Mokhtada Asadar and his supporters do have much more militant rethoric than the Grand Ayatollah but they have essentially joint his call for direct elections to decide the future of the country. This was opposition to the American plan to select a transitional government something the Shiites feel is too much control in American hands. There are suspitions too about the Kurdish demands for a federal system;the fear is that this one plea to split the country rather than uniting it. So strong and competing demands for what Iraq should be like but leaders from all sides said the key thing is that the transitional government should be seen to be legitimate and if it is not than it will be even weaker than the current arrangement for Iraqi authorities.

21 January 2004 Thursday

The chief US administrator in Iraq Paul Bremer visited New York for talks with the UN Secretary General Kofi Annan. There is growing criticism of Washington's plan for the return to Iraqi sovereignity by the end of June 2004 without direct elections. The whole story with the elections is the fear of the Shiite majority they could be dominated by the Suni minority as it was under Saddam. The Americans hope UN support would hault the clamor from Iraq's majority Shiites who demonstrated again in Baghdad that day to demand an elected government. The growing opposition to Washington's plans for handing power to the Iraqis has led it to return to the UN. The Americans want the UN to back their hand-over plan which consists of indirect elections to a new assembly which will than choose the government. They hope an UN stamp of approval would hault criticism from the majority Shiite community and particularly from the most influencial cleric Ayatollah Sistani who's calling for direct elections. The UN Secretary General Kofi Annan will hold talks with the US administrator for Iraq Paul Bremer and members of the Iraqi governing council. The Japanese prime minister Junichiro Koizumi has again defended his decision to send troops to Iraq to take part in humanitarian activities. He told Parliament that Japan should contribute agressively to the reconstruction of Iraq because its own future depended on a stable and prosperous world. He said although Iraq was not a safe place for Japanese soldiers they've been trained properly to work in difficult environment.

22 January 2004

23 January 2004 Friday

2 US military pilots died when their helicopter was shot down in Northern Iraq. Several other people were killed in Iraq in attacks on American forces and on Iraqis who'd worked for them. 3 Iraqi women cleaners died in a gun-attack on their mini-bus in Fallujah and 3 US soldiers were killed in Bakuba by Iraqi gunmen.

The Director of the CIA George Tenneth has announced that his special advisor on Iraq's weapons' program David Kay has resigned. David Kay's team in Iraq has so far failed to find any weapons of mass destruction despite the assurances of Tony Blair for such weapons. An UN-team has arrived in Iraq to start preparations for a possible return of UN international staff who're withdrawn following the devastating attack on the UN headquarters in Baghdad in August 2003. The team's arrival comes as the Americans wait a decision from the UN on whethter to study the visibility of direct elections in the next 4 months or so. The whole story with the Iraqi elections is the fear of the Shiite majority not to be dominated by the Suni minority as it was under Saddam. The giant American oil services company Halliburton has dismissed 2 employees accused of taking bribes for contracts to supply American troops in Iraq. The latest claim concerned a contract by Halliburton to provide a variety of oil supplies to US troops in Iraq.

24 January 2004 Saturday

13 American troops have been killed in separate bomb attacks in Iraq. The US military command said the US soldiers died hit their convoy near the town of Fallujah west of the Capital Baghdad-an area of frequent attacks against Ameri can forces. Earlier the US military said 4 Iraqis have been killed in a car bomb attack in the town of Samarra which lies to the north of the Iraqi capital. The Samarra bomb attack was close to the police headquarters and thetown council building. According to a US military police spokesman it happened as an American patrol was turning into the police station. It's believed to be a remote controlled bomb and it threw the vehicle in the air, left a deep crater, damaged a number of other cars and scattered glass over a wide area. The death toll rose to 3 during the morning and 7 Americans who're in the council building were among the casualties with minor injuries. A Sammarra police official described it as "sabotage aimed at terrorizing people and spreading chaos". Later came the news that 2 more American soldiers have been killed when their convoy struck a road side bomb north of Falluja. In Haladiya some other Amis were deprived of their lives (CNN, BBC)

25 January 2004 Sunday

An American military helicopter crashed into river Tigris while on patrol over the northern Iraqi town of Mosul;2 Iraqi policemen and the translator were instantly killed. The cause of the helicopter crash is still not known. The cause of the helicopter crash 2 days earlier also is still not known.

26 January 2004 Monday

Senator David Kay said to the New York Times, "it was well known that Iraq had actually no weapons of mass destruction, but we were set on to go to war in Iraq. It was more intelligence failure and now John Tenneth-the CIA Director-is in the hot seat and not President Bush." David Kay too advocated the war against Iraq and now will be forced to resign over the scandal;
"...the Lybian announcement of hidden weapons of mass destruction undetected by the CIA was just another scandal", he said. The US Secretary of State Collin Powel visiting Moscow after the yesterday's inauguration of Georgian President Michael Saakashvilli also defended the US decision to make a war on Iraq: "The risc was to big to allow Iraq and Saddam Hussein to head on in the same direction", he said to the CNN.

At the same time 2 American soldiers were killed when a road side bomb ex ploded when their mini-bus was passing along this freqently used street in Baghdad. The official number of US soldiers killed after the war end in April 2003 is now well above 600. Even after the capture of Saddam Hussein in December 2003 by the Americans the number of attacks on US targits is over 140, CNN said. Saddam is kept in a secrete place in Iraq but officially the former president is n o t indicted.

26 January 2004 Monday

The President of Afghanistan's transitional government Hamid Karzai has signed the country's new constitution 3 weeks after it was aproved by the Grand Assembly or Loya Jirga. The signing ceremony in Kabul was attended by Afghan government ministers and ambassadors from around the world. The constitution invisages a strong Presidency and enshrines eqaul rights for men and women. During the signing ceremony in the Afghani foreign ministry marble hall Hamid Karzai was given a golden pen by the Afghan King Zahir Shah to sign with, as shown on BBC-screen.

27 January 2004 Tuesday

A Canadian soldier died when a suicide bomber flunged himself under his vehicle. 3 other Canadians were injured. The suicide bomber flunged himself under the vehicle when the convoy on a patrol slowed down for a speed bump. Later on this day the Taleban claimed responsibility for the attack. Canada has some 2, OOO sodliers spread over Afghanistan.

27 January 2004 Tuesday

In the Iraqi town of Haladiya a mighty road side bomb exploded killing 3 Americans and wounding several others.2 Iraqis were also killed. The attack occured in an area known as the Suni Triangle-a stronghold of opposition to the American led coalition. This day was really a black day for the Americans in occupied Iraq: 8 Americans were killed in 3 separate attacks in Kandaliya near Baghdad and a CNN-team of 2 was also killed. At the same time the UN is considering to send a team to Baghdad to assess the conditions for elections in Iraq! It is so ridicule, so stupid, so laughable: on one hand is absolutely visible that elections are not possible in Iraq; on the other hand is not clear the status of the new would-be government: federal or national government? Elections or selections??

27 January 2004 Tuesday

The Pakistani authorities have confirmed they're still questioning 7 senior nuclear scientists first detained a week earlier in connection with the probe in the possible transfer of information on nuclear weapons' technology. Those been questioned include the man widely regarded as the father of the Pakistani nuclear bomb-Dr. Abdul Kadir Khan. The secrete investigation began 2 months earlier after the UN Nuclear Agency-the IAEA-shared with Pakistan information gathered from Iran and Lybia about their nuclear programs.

28 January 2004 Wendesday

A British soldier was killed and 3 others injured in Kabul when a suicide bomber drove his taxi into a patrol convoy.

28 January 2004

In central Baghdad 3 Iraqis were killed when a bomb went off near hotel used frequently by foreigners.

29 January 2004 Thursday

7 Americans were killed by a remote control bomb in the Iraqi city of Bakuba.

31 January 2004

The German defence Minister Peter Struck inspected the German troops stationed around the city of Kunduz where his propeller-plane landed safely in the sunny Saturday afternoon. Struck announced his decision to increase the number of the German teams working in Afghanistan from 8 to 16. Special attention was paid to the reconstruction of streets and high ways.

Pakistan has dismissed its top nuclear scientist Kadir Khan from his post as advisor to the prime minister. Mr. Khan-regarded as the father of the Pakistani nuclear bomb program-was one of several people questioned by the authorities in connection with possible transfer of nuclear weapons technology from Pakistan to other countries such as Lybia and North Korea.

31 January 2004 Saturday

2 major EU airlines have cancelled a number of flights to the US over security fears. British Airways said it cancelled 3 of its flights to the US on the advice of the British government;a few hours later Air France announced it have also cancelled 2 Washington-bound flights. The cancellations came after a warning from US-officials that they have new intelligence that BA & Air France flights might be highjacked and crashed into targets in the US. The US-Department of Homeland Security said they remained concerned about the desire of Al Qaida to target aviation, esp. international aviation. A spokes man said US-intelligence continued to gather specific credible threat information on international flights and they are acting on the bases of that. This is similar but not identical to the alert cancelled a number of flights over the Christmas and New-Year-holiday. Once again British Airways flight 223 from London to Washington appears to be the focus of particular concern. But the cancellation of Paris-Washington and London-Miami flights is new.

31 January 2004 Saturday

A car bomb attack on a police station in the Northern Iraqi city of Mosul has killed 10 people, 44 others were injured in the blast which occured close to a bus stop at a busy time of the morning. Eye-witness accounts suggested it was yet another suicide attack targetting those working with the US-led coalition.

01 February 2004

More than 107 people have been killed in Northern Iraq by suicide bombers who attacked the offices of the 2 main rival Kurdish political parties in the city of Erbil. Kurdish officials were quated to say they fear the number of death can go much higher. The suicide bombers blew themselves up in crowded offices filled with people who had come to greet Kurdish officials on the first day of the Muslim holiday Eadel-Atha. Witnesses described scenes of chaos, the authorities called on citizens to donate blood and doctors to return from their holiday. Bodies were taken away on lorries. The 2 bombers walked into the branch offices of the Kurdistan Democratic Party and the Patriotic Union of Kurdistan - the main factions Iraq's Kurdish North. Security was lax because of the festive season and many senior officials were present some of them were said to be among the casualties.

The Polish military in Iraq said 20 Iraqis were killed in an explosion at a munitions depot about 180 km South-West of Kerbala. The depot was under the protection of Polish soldiers of the coalition forces. A Polish officer said around 20 Iraqis succeeded in getting in into a fortified building in the munitions depot in the early hours of the morning and soon afterward it exploded. The Iraqi intruders were detected by radar but the Polish soldiers guarding the site were unable to stop them. First reports suggested they could have been trying to loot weapons stored at the depot-small arms, mortars and rockets and they often have been targeted by looters in the past.

8 February 2004 Sunday

On a conference in the Capital Kabul the Afghan government said the opium production last year acounted for 90% of heroin consuption in Europe despite the Afghan government's efforts to curb production since the fall of Taleban. Officials fear profits from the drug help to finance terrorists groups. There have been a lot of views on this conference on how best to dismantle Afghanistan's opium economy. The problem now threatens Afghanistan's political and economic future. Adam Burlakos of the UN office on drugs and crime said, this an essential issue to address if you go seriously to things like stability in the provinces but they all can be negatively impacted by the very signifficant opium economy. Many drugs control experts now admit the issue was neglected after the fall of Taleban in 2002. The war on terror took precedence.

08 February 2004

The former Chief UN weapons inspector Hans Blicks said the USA and Britain were not sufficiently critical of their intelligence on Iraq because they were already convinced Saddam Hussein possessed weapons of mass destruction. Speaking to the BBC Hans Blicks said "the search for weapons has become a witch hunt". He said there has been too much reliance and exaggerated information from Iraqi defectors and intelligence had been misinterpreted: "We had the wrong intelligence. They listened very much to defectors and many of the defectors and many of the defectors were exaggerating things. There was missing all the way through from the intelligence and from the goverments a critical thinking. They were so sure that Iraq "had" weapons of mass destruction that it was like a witch hunt;if you are convinced that there are witches than you'll take every broom that you see at the corner as an evidence of existing of such witches", he stressed. Hans Blicks said that he believed although President Bush and the British prime minister Tony Blair had acted in a good faith he said they've embellished the case for war against Iraq.

08 February 2004

The American appointed governing council in Iraq has been meeting an UN delegation to discuss whether elections can be held by June 2004. The talks mark the start of intensive UN consultations with the various Iraqi factions. The UN fact-finding team lead by its former envoy to Afghanistan Lakhdar Brahimi is trying to break an empass between the Americans and Iraq's Shiite clergy over transition to self-rule.

The Japanese troop contingent crossed into Iraq from Quwait-the first Japanese troop contingent sent to Iraq on a humanitarian mission. They are also the first Japanese soldiers to be deployed in an area of conflicts since the WW_2 under a controversial legislation enacted in Japan in 2003. Critics in Japan have argued that the move violates Japan's pacifist constitution. At the same time a bomb explosion at a police station in Baghdad killed 3 US troops 11 others were wounded.

09 February 2004

The interim Afghan president Hamed Kharzai appealed to the Afghan people to stop producing opium and opium buds from which heroin is easiliy made. 75% of the heroin used in Europe and 25% of the heroin used in the US has an Afghan origin. The former Taleban regime in Afghanistan has banned the opium production but it flurished up again after the fall of the Taleban in 2002. Some neighbouring countries-such as Iran and Pakistan-have an iron grip on opium production and on the ground of religious and juridical consideration opium is practically not produced in these 2 countries.

10 February 2004

The UN top official for fighting drug trafficking has called for foreign troops in Afghanistan to target smugglers and drug-making laboratories there. Antonio Mario da Costa told the conference in Kabul that the American raid on an opium processing laboratories in January-of which we heard nothing-had a big impact and should be repeated throughout the country. But correspondents said US and NATO forces have resisted calles from the Afghan government to tackle drug traffickers and have concentrated instead on maintaining security.

75% of the world opium was produce in Afghanistan last year and the UN and other agencies have warned that Afghanistan riscs becoming economically dependent on the drug trade.

10 February 2004

A mighty car bomb explosion in the front of police station killed 15 people and injured 40 others in the city of Iskandariya 40km northwest from Baghdad. The attack aimed and hit American-trained Iraqi policemen which are mostly hated as renegades.

With this attack the number of the killed Iraqis in bomb attacks rose to 300 since the end of thewar. Eye-witnisses said there were pools of blood which had to be washed away. The attack occured about lunch time. Some accused the Americans of been heavy-handed for not allowing relatives of those killed or injured to help their relatives. Other sources claimed the attack was planted by the Americans themselves to stage a future impact on Al Qaida;whether this is true will be shown by the future.

11 February 2004

47 Iraqis were killed in a suicide bomb attack in the capital Baghdad, scores of others were wounded. The suicide bomber drove his car into a queue of men waiting alongside the road at a police station to apply for jobs at police and army; than he detonated his explosives converting his car into volcan of deadly shrapnels. The exact dead toll is not exactly known but this is the price the Iraqis have to pay for their cooperation to the Americans and the Americans for the arrest of Saddam Hussein on 13th of December 2003 in Tikrita deadly spade of deadly attacks of Saddam loyalists who don't want to see their country conquered by the invador. This is the second deadly attack on American troops in the past 2 days.

12 February 2004

A senior American commander and member of the US General Staff in Iraq escaped unharmed when his convoy came under Iraqi rocket fire. The Americans returned the fire which allowed General John Abi Zaid to escape unharmed to his headquarters. General Abi Zaid who is the Head of the American Central Command in Iraq was in a convoy of vehicles in the city of Fallujah when his car came under fire of rocket-propelled grenades. An American spokesman said no one was injured but this was not what we saw on TV-screen: 5 minutes of skirmeshes with Iraqi guerrilas.

Earlier a UN envoy held discussions about the future of Iraq with the senior Shiite Muslim cleric Grand Ayatollah Ali al Sistani when the rocket attack came. The envoy-Lakhdar Brahimi-said the UN agreed with the Ayatollah on the need of elections but added they should be held in the best possible conditions. Actually this piece of news was only repeated by the media to overshadow the rocket attack on the Head of the American Central Command in Iraq General John Abizaid.

Abizzee

Abbizay

Abi Zaid

13 February 2004 Friday

One US soldier was shot dead by the Iraqis when he was on patrol in the capital Baghdad.

14 February 2004

19 people were killed in Fallujah when Iraqi gunmen opened fire at a police station with mortars and machine guns. The number of the wounded is not known yet.

****

Jam Mohamed Khan - provincial governor of Uruzgan province north of Kandahar

Andrew North - BBC correspondent in Afghanistan in 2004

Char-Chino - a district of Uruzgan province in Afghanistan where 11 civilians were killed by a US air raid

Brian Healthety - US military spokesman in Afghanistan; lt. colonnel

this is a good to hang the story on - oporen punkt

Catrine Gun - former employee of British Intelligence Gathering Center

26-04-1894 - Rudolf Hess born

JCHQ - British Intelligence Gathering Center

Moqtada al sadar - Iraqi radical cleric with chances to win the elections if any

George Tenneth - CIA Director

David Kay - CIA special advisor on Iraqi weapons' programme

Halliburton - a giant American oil services company which supplied the Pentagon with oil during the Iraqi war on increased prices;former subsidiary of the Vice President Dick Chayne;accused of taking bribes for contracts to supply American troops in Iraq.

Paul Bremer- chief US administrator for Iraq

Sistani - Ayatollah, most influential Shiite cleric, calling fordirect elections.

Junichiro Koizumi - Japanese prime minister, sent Japanese troops to Iraq

Chinese White, Crocodile Snow Powder - a mighty drug, stronger than heroin made for medical anaestetic

Kylie Morris - BBC correspondent to Thailand

David Burn - EU health commissioner, visited Thailand in January 2004

Mike Woodridge - BBC correspondent in Iraq

Kushid Mahmud Masuri - Pakistani foreign minister
Kursid Mahmood Kussuri - Pakistani foreign minister
Kursid Kassuri - Pakistani foreign minister

Rachel Harvey - BBC correspondent in Thailand
26 January 2004-interim Afghan President Hamid Karzai signed the new Constitution in the presence of ambassadors all around the world
Andrew North - BBC correspondent in Afghanistan
Abdul Kadir Khan - Dr., father of the Pakistani nuclear bomb
Barbara Plett - BBC correspondent in Baghdad
Mike Woodridge - BBC_correspondent in Baghdad
Adam Burlakos-from the UN office on drugs and crime
Andrew North-BBC correspondent on the Afghan conference on opium in Kabul on O8 Feb 2004
Antonio Mario Costa-the UN top official for fighting drug trafficking
Pongthep Thepkanchana - Thailand's justice minister

$$$$$$$

< IRAQ . TXT >

1O JAN 2OO3 35OOO US troops sent to The Gulf
11 JAN 2OO3 27OOO US troops sent to The Gulf
2O JAN 26OOO UK troops & 12O tanks
21 JAN 37OOO US troops
15 FEB 2OO3 15O OOO US troops estimated
O9-O9 2OO3 1O 5OO British troops in Iraq plus 2 new bataillons to send

The American desire is from the Northern front in Turkey to distroy Iraq:
finally this plan failed and the American invasion began from the South.

< IRAQ-E1.TXT >
In a special BBC-Interview today 2O Nov at 1O:OO GMT the Iraqi representative Mustafa Adami said: " Not Iraq but the USA posses weapons of mass distruction; and not only posses them but also used them in Hiroshima and in Vietnam and in Iraq used depleted uranium. On the concience of the US Presidents lay the death of 1 7OO OOO peaceful Iraqi civilists who died from starvation and radiation in the years after the Golf war 1991. In Yugoslavia-not in Kosovo-the Amricans didn't hesitate to bombard kindergartens, hospitals, senior homes, embassies and TV-stations". After this words Mustafa Adami was interrupted by the BBC-moderator Elizabeth Doucet who speaks with a sharp voice and stinging brogue-accent. Also on BBC on 19 NOV at 15:OO GMT the Bulgarian journalist Iwo Indzhew praised the new-comers to the NATO. Iwo Indzhew, who has rather weak voice and rather bad English boasted himself

to be a comentator at the Bulgarian Television BTV. He praised the newcomers to the NATO-club with the following example: " When an ill man goes to the dentist he goes not for love to the dentist but because he needs him for his treatment". Iwo Indzhev failed to elaborate if the new comers do need such a "dentist" and how expensive such a depleting medication will coast to the news comers. He failed to compare the also with Austria and with Switzerland, who do existist already 53 years without the NATO-"therapy".

< IRAQ . TXT >

10 JAN 2003 35000 US troops sent to The Gulf
11 JAN 2003 27000 US troops sent to The Gulf
20 JAN 26000 UK troops & 120 tanks
21 JAN 37000 US troops
15 FEB 2003 150 000 US troops estimated
09-09 2003 10 500 British troops in Iraq plus 2 new bataillons to send

The American desire is from the Northern front in Turkey to distroy Iraq: finally this plan failed and the American invasion began from the South.

The foreign minister of the Northern Alliance Abdulah Abdulah said the Northern Alliance had asked formally the UN to to establish broad based multiethnic goverment in Afghanistan. George Bush was pleased with the development in Afghanistan and called the Northern Alliance to observe human rights there. Later this day it became clear that American special forces were operating in Kabul. The former president Rabani gave an interview in the Arabic TV al Jezira in which he said that in the new Goverment the former King had an important role to play.

< IRAQ . TXT >

10 JAN 2003 35000 US troops sent to The Gulf
11 JAN 2003 27000 US troops sent to The Gulf
20 JAN 26000 UK troops & 120 tanks
21 JAN 37000 US troops
15 FEB 2003 150 000 US troops estimated
09-09 2003 10 500 British troops in Iraq plus 2 new bataillons to send

The American desire is from the Northern front in Turkey to distroy Iraq: finally this plan failed and the American invasion began from the South.

< IRAQ-E1.TXT >
In a special BBC-Interview today 20 Nov at 10:00 GMT the Iraqi representative Mustafa Adami said: " Not Iraq but the USA posses weapons of mass distruction; and not only posses them but also used them in Hiroshima and in Vietnam and in Iraq used depleted uranium. On the concience of the US Presidents lay the death of 1 700 000 peaceful Iraqi civilists

who died from starvation and radiation in the years after the Golf war 1991. In Yugoslavia-not in Kosovo-the Amricans didn't hesitate to bombard kindergartens, hospitals, senior homes, embassies and TV-stations". After this words Mustafa Adami was interrupted by the BBC-moderator Elizabeth Doucet who speaks with a sharp voice and stinging brogue-accent. Also on BBC on 19 NOV at 15:OO GMT the Bulgarian journalist Iwo Indzhew praised the new-comers to the NATO. Iwo Indzhew, who has rather weak voice and rather bad English boasted himself to be a comentator at the Bulgarian Television BTV. He praised the newcomers to the NATO-club with the following example: " When an ill man goes to the dentist he goes not for love to the dentist but because he needs him for his treatment". Iwo Indzhev failed to elaborate if the new comers do need such a "dentist" and how expensive such a depleting medication will coast to the news comers. He failed to compare the also with Austria and with Switzerland, who do existist already 53 years without the NATO-"therapy".

< IRAQ . TXT >

1O JAN 2OO3 35OOO US troops sent to The Gulf
11 JAN 2OO3 27OOO US troops sent to The Gulf
2O JAN 26OOO UK troops & 12O tanks
21 JAN 37OOO US troops
15 FEB 2OO3 15O OOO US troops estimated
O9-O9 2OO3 1O 5OO British troops in Iraq plus 2 new bataillons to send

The American desire is from the Northern front in Turkey to distroy Iraq: finally this plan failed and the American invasion began from the South.

May & June 2008

Speaking to the Israeli Kneset President Bush urged the Arab nations and esp. Saudi Arabia to increase the oil output up to 300,000 barrels a day to suppress oil prices below the $120 bench mark. But by end of June oil was already $146.

The American Petrol Funds stated "this is possible" but also "oil is the best commodity to invest money in". Iran by contrast said "the oil price will surpass the $200 bench mark" inviting the American Petrol Funds' laughter to the despising comment "Iran will hock on its oil waiting for its $200 a barrel while realistically the oil price subsided already from $126 to beneath $120 a barrel". Iran, Russia and Qatar-the world's richest gas countries decided to unify into a gas cartel similar to the OPEK.

An US soldier was disciplined for using the holly book of Quran as a target practice. His commander-a general of the 4th infantery division in Northern Baghdad apologized publicly in the front of tv cameras by a synchronized translation into Arabic, saying "this soldier has been removed from the staff of our 4th infantery division, from all his commanding posts & from

Baghdad..." as shown by the CNN. The senior al Qaida leader in Mosul Ahmed Ali Ahmed was sentenced to death and executed for his role in the kidnapping and murdering the catholic archbishop of Mosul in February 2008.

The oil price hit $133, - a barrel.

Scott McLarren- press secry. of Pres. Bush-published a new book criticizing the President of stirring emotions instead facts before whirling the country into the Iraqi war without sufficient preparations. Mr. Bush thanked him formally.

McLarren accused him-informally-already 2 years ago when he stepped down that the Iraq war was ill-planned and doomed to ground down from the very beginning. The number of US soldiers who committed suicide reached 155 only in the last year. But the CIA-Chief Director Michael Hayden declared "al Qaida is defeated both in Iraq and Saudi Arabia and the goals of the war are satisfactorily fulfilled." He said nothing about the trial of Michael Greyson which started in California; he's accused of murdering 21 Iraqi civilians in 2005. More similar trials are expected.

June 2008

The oil price reached $145, - a barrel.

Japan called upon the world community to take coordinated measures to stop the headlong escalation of the oil price. The OPEK however refused to increase oil output in order to stop the price escalation. Japan, China, India & the U.S. are the biggest oil importer of the world. In the US the gasoline price hit $4.oo a gallon and many factories transformed to 4-days week in order to spare travel costs of their workers. 3% of the workers gave in their private cars and switched over to public US-transport. In Slovenia President Bush did not speak on oil:he advocated for Turkey to become EU-member though the US is not its member;he demanded Turkey to get EU-member despite its poor economic & human rights' records. Turkey is oil self-sufficient & produces the US fighter jets F-16. In Slovenia Bush critisized the Iranian nuclear program, did not discus EU-problems. After his speech Iran started to withdraw its assets from EU-banks which hit financially the EU-economy after the oil crisis.

The Iraqi president al Malakhi negotiated with the U.S. to give it permanent military bases on Iraqi soil. Iran protested vigorously against the agreement "which will allow the Americans to attack Iranian targets from Iraqi soil". Israel too said "the war with Iran is inevitabl and it will attack Iranian targets to disrupt the Iranian nuclear program; Israel will not tolerate atomic program so close to its borders". Presidential wife Laura Bush-went to Afghanistan for a meeting with the Afghan president Hamed Karzai. A car bomb went off and killed the leader of the Saddam Hussein's tribe leader Ali Ahmadi north-west from Baghdad facing some Western greetings. US-president George Bush spoke on a meeting in Slovenia and demanded "the EU to accept Turkey in its ranks" despite its poor record on human rights; Turkey congratulated his demand.

US air force destroyed Pakistani frontier base & killed 11 Pakistani soldiers & 40 civilians in Pactica province; "it wasn't mistake", US command commented. Paki stan protested in vain, Afghanistan sent in reinforcement troops. A truck-bomb in Kandahar blew up in the front of the prison and 350 Taleban prisoners managed to escape to freedom as "a fresh blood to the Taleban resistence". In his 2 days' visit to London President Bush said "there is no definitive term to withdraw US from Iraq". The term initially set was by April 2008, than prolonged to November 2008 and agreed upon for 2011.

In a desperate hatred Bush asked the world to increase oil output which seems already impossible because of the US adventures. Shell stopped its Niger ian production of 200,000 barrels daily because of rebels'attacks on Shell-instalations. Further 120,000 barrels daily production were blocked for Shevron in a rebels'blockade by the MEN. Saudi Arabia oil minister promised to increase the output to the end of the year but the OPEK-president Hakib Khalil rejected his proposal.

September-October 2008

After the oil price reached the pick of $168 a barrel the OPEC countries met in Vienna and decided to reduce output to keep prices high. As to the London bus attack on 07-07-2005 an University study showed that many details were exaggerated or even freely thought out to make it easier for the general modest public to believe into the story and to go down better with:the alleged bus CCTV never existed and the police computer reconstruction was falsified, said BBC on 10-09-2008 at 12.oo CET.

In Pakistan Assad Ali Azidari was sworn in as a new president after the resignation of Pervaze Musharraf. He's husband of the assassinated Benazir Bhutto. He promised to develop good & friendly relations with his neighbours. But in North West Pakistan American planes bombarded barbarically villages and killed civilians. In one single bombardment the number of the victims was 90 civilians. The Pentagon sent in a special envoy to clarify the murder: "To us were reported only 7", he said.2 US helicopters were downed in Baghdad. Iran forced an American spy plane to land. The Pentagon dismissed any knowledge of it : "The plane was a Hungarian one", it said.

The US military killed Abdul Kaswara -al Qaida 2nd of command in Iraq. He managed to preserve the entire al Qaida net work in northern Iraq. He was killed in a battle in Mosul with 5 other al Qaida fighters. US helicopter from North Iraq raided neighbouring Syria, killed 8 civilians 5 of them children as the video showed. Syria protested sharply against the unprovoked attack both to the Iraq & to the US, lodged a formal letter of "protest & condemnation of the barbaric US terrorism" to the UN-Security Council and shut down the American school & the American cultural centre in Damascus. US military said "this was the 7 or the 8th attack of

Syrian targets approved and signed by Colin Powell and President Bush. A US spokesman said "the attack was carried out by US special forces and they had fulfilled their task successfully". A day later a drinking water pipe line was blown up depriving 700,000 Baghdadis of drinking water:the terrorists pretended to repair the water pipe line but indeed they implanted the bomb and than detonated it from a safe distance. Omar ben Laden-son of Osama ben Laden asked Spain for political asylum after he was forbidden to live in Britain with his British wife. Ayman al Zawahri was the last political leader to take a stand to the election of Barack Obama for an US President; he insulted him and critisized him "for forgetting his "Muslim & Kenian roots"". State Department spokesman Sean McCormack dismissed his 23 minutes internet speech as "despicable terrorist comments".

In Iraq the oil concern Shell started preparations for producing earth gas;up till now it was burnt away or re-injected back into the soil. Russian Ambassador to Washington said "Russian reaction in Georgia is equivalent to the American 09-11-2001". The Americans did not reject affront escalating oil prices, simply kept quite. Affronting the global finance chaos-as presidential candidate Barack Obama put it 14 days after me-nobody was able or willing to remember the same resembling chaos of the 1930ies and the German Gruender years of the 1870ies. The US President George W. Bush put it "no pay loans will rose (instead of rise) and no global economy'll rose unless we accept this $700,000,000,000 bail out package". The package was voted & accepted by Congress & Bush signed it into law on a late Friday night to prevent the competition of Asian share markets. Europe was not united and only the Dutch government bailed out 40 bn euro worth of the joint Dutch-Belgian-Luxemburg banking-financial group Fortis. Belgium and Luxemburg refused to bail it out. Paul Krugman received the Nobel price for economy;in his book he critisized fiercely President Bush and his numerous blunders during the war. The former Republican secretary of state in the Bush administration Collin Powel endorsed and supported publicly the democratic presidential candidate Barack Obama: "Obama is more flexible;he can better manage the current economic situation & respond correctly to the current economic challenges", said Powel in a tv-interview though he himself is a Republican & friend of President Bush.

Island nationalized its ailing stocks by 14,000,000 euro but Scandinavia and EU didn't follow. Later Island received $5 bn from Russia. German Chancellor Angela Merkel-by priest back ground & education-refused "to give out a blank check to the banks" and "united" Europe failed to unite to buy out the "toxic debts" of the ailing EU-banks & finance groups over the national boundaries. With French President Nicholas Sarkozy she arranged an agreement "not to prop up swaying present branches suffocating by toxic debts but to invest in new more profitable industries and technologies. The British finance minister Alistair Darling reass ured Parliament of the stability of the British economy: "We still have 500,000 vacant jobs", he stated.

The crisis provoked Pope Benedict to state "money is unpredictable but love into God is eternal!". BBC sr.commentator Julian Marshall (not the economist Marshall Gold) asked "how strong is Al Qaida now & how to compete with it where no debts & loans are available" &

he got "answer" from his underneath BBC-Owen Benneth Jones-"al Qaida is down but not out!" BBC put it "the global financial crises in US & EU will lead to a drop of international oil demand which hurt badly several post-war oil empires including George W. Bush' one. The Brits started to live on 5 pounds a day as a Brit lady journalist put it to the BBC.

Pres. Bush called the financial crisis melt down, presidential candidate Barack Obama named it a mess, BBC-free fall but I was 14 days earlier to name it a sheer catastrophy and full chaos repeated later by so many journalists & agencies.

The crisis started with the collapse of the Lehmann Brothers financial group followed by Washington Mutual. Than Pres. Bush ordered a $700 bn bail out to flush the crises to Europe and succeeded partly. Island collapsed despite governmental bail out of $14 bn-the bank debts exceeded 9 times its actual GDP. Countries and governments across Europe worked frantically on the weekends to pass bills, bails & laws overturned by reality already the very next day; negotiating nights to overspeed Asian share & stock markets unable to re-capitalize the whole of value exceeded. EU-Banks limited guaranty on private savings to 50, ooo euro equal to $68,000. The British government put a $90 bn rescue package;BBC called it "semi-nationalization". The German bail-out amounted to 130 bn euro. Hungary received 14 bn euro from the IMF and 9bn from the EU. Japan pumped into its economy $214 bn. The Japanese prime minister Tara Aso called the financial crises "financial typhoon" and "one in century event". France and Britain came up with a common strategy and urged China & the oil countries to inject more cash into the world economy.

Barack Obama named it mess
BBC - free fall
President Bush - melt down
I myself - global catastrophy
. . . . . . - chaos
the president of the Federal Reserve - financial tsunami
the Japanese prime minister Tara Aso-financial typhoon & one in a century event
Martin King, Director of The Bank of England-total collapse of the bank system

The "global financial melt-down"-as G.W. Bush put it-"more over its US bail-out needs a while" and caused more trouble and destruction than the entire bloody senseless Iraq war which claimed over 200,000 human lives in vain. It will be come obvious-the more and the more-that the whole Iraqi war was financed in a foul way under the dictatorship of George W. Bush-the huge oil magnate, Senator & dictator of Texas who came to power in wrigged elections in 1999-less oil & more blood for the whole world: even the Vatican condemned him before the end of his mandate. In a very nervous voice victorious Bush said "we don't know if Osama ben Laden is in a cave or otherwise else but we know for sure he is not in charge of Afghanistan anymore". Great success indeed. On G-7 meeting during the week end he acknowledged "the global financial crisis is a very serious crisis indeed and its needs very serious global solutions in every sector of economy".

The British government awarded a soldier with the Victorian cross for braver-a British veteran from the Vietnam war. Prince Harry was forced to apologize in public for insulting 2006 on video tape his fellow soldiers calling them "paki" and "tinty".

This is not the end of the story yet-an 8 years criminal saga of US & presidential crimes esp. of W. Bush whose dynasty father George Bush senior was shot in the brain in the 1980ies; than he was Reagan's defence minister. Now in a hastily and suddenly organized press conference in Baghdad President George W. Bush was attacked too:an Iraqi journalist took off his shoes, threw them at Bush and hit him successfully in his face. For the Muslims the shoes are something very derogative and despicable, a very great and deep insult. The journalist was arrested, beaten and sentenced to 15 years of prison according "the Iraqi law of insulting foreigners".

Abdul Kaswara-al Qaida second in command of Iraq, killed in October 2008
Abdul Kaswara-al Qaida second in command of Iraq, killed in October 2008
Alistair Darling-British finance minister
Malcolm X-American leader in 1960: "symbol of anti-imperialism"(CNN, BBC, Yahoo)
Paul Krugman-Nobel price winner for economy;critisized fiercely Bush & his war
16-the number of the Iraqi suicide bomb teenagers in 2008 alone.
Benchly Park-British museum of computing in London developed greatly by IBM Assad Ali Azidari-new Pakistani president, husband of the assassinated former president Benazir Bhutto daughter of 1979 hanged president Sulficar Ali Bhutto
GDP-gross domestic product bail=money paid by/for a person accused of a crime to get temporarily released
bail out =rescue from financial difficulties:(Oxford dictionary, 1989, p.77).
Christine l'Ugan-Luxemburg bank meeting spokes person
Papillon-virus to cause some cancers;its discoverer got Nobel price for it
Paul Krugman-economy Nobelist;fiercely critisized Pres. Bush for his war blunders
Tara Aso-Japanese prime minister
Hamada-Japanese defence minister
Temogami-Japanese air forces chief of staff;sacked in October 2008
Omar ben Laden-son of Osama ben Laden-left Britain;asked Spain for polit.asylum Fortis-a joint Dutch-Belgian-Luxemburg banking-financial group

* * *

"Warfares only waste human lives", Confucius 500 B.C.
Ali Ahmadi-Saddam's tribe leader killed by a car bomb on 10-06-2008
Ashua Afghani- Afghan financial minister
Ali Naim Naimi- Saudi Arabia oil minister
Tartar Motors-Indian car producer of world's cheapest car-under $2ooo
Scott McLarren- Bush'press secry. Criticized him for his numerous war blunders
Laura Bush- President's Bush wife

MEN=movement for emancipation of Nigeria; abolished the slavery in 1995

Hakib Khalil-OPEK president

Abdul Kaswara -al Qaida 2nd of command in Iraq; killed in October 2008

Ayman al Zawahri-al Qaida 2nd after Abdul Kaswara

al Gezeera-Qatar based Arabic television channel

Algeciras-Spanish city just opposite to the Moroccan port of Tanger

Sean McCormack-spokesman of the State Department in November 2008

McCain, .. - unsuccessful Republican presidential candidate in 2008

McCain, Mark - CNN journalist

paki – a British army derogative insult to Pakistani fellow soldiers

tinty – a British army derogative insult to dark-skinned fellow soldiers

Nancy Pallosy-speaker of the House of the representatives in 2008

Thomas Summers-Obama's economic adviser

07-07-2005 Thursday

At midday 4 suicide bombers detonated their bombs in 3 under ground trains of the London tube and in one bus. The death toll amounted to 55 people killed and 33 missing. The injured were over 1,200 people.

Many of the victims were foreign tourists visiting London. British Prime Minister Tony Blair surrounded by US President George W. Bush and French Prime Minister Jacque Chirac ddenounced sharply the terrorist and said in short TV interview "the terrorist will not defeat the British campaign in Iraq neither the British public live"

The Conservatives by contrast critisized sharply the Chief of the Metropolitan Police Ion Blair. Italy stated "it will withdraw its troops from Iraq by September 2005". Many countries extended their condolence to Britain, among them Spain - the country which most suffered of such kind of terror attacks on trains in Madrid in March 2004 when 199 people died and Spain withdrew immediately its troop from Iraq as result.

France and Britain increased their stage of alert from orange to red but the US made no changes. A day later 20,000 people were evacuated from Birmingam because of a bomb threat which turned out to be a false one. In Germany the trains of the Berlin tube were also stopped for several hours-without any practical need or result-until the situation became clear. In Leeds 1,200 people were evacuated when British police raided the home of the suspected terrorists and found there essential amount of explosives but no written remarks. Finally it became clear that "these were suicide attacks because it was not possible to use mobile phones in the tube as detonators as initially suspected. The suicide bombers intended to produce a burning cross accross London", the metropolitan police statement read "now we have to produce new form of relationship with the Muslim community", continued the state ment. The British Muslim

Counil denounced sharply the terrorist bombing of the London tube saying "this had nothing to do with the genuin Islam!" Nontheless senior Muslim-cleric Zakhir Badawi-was prohibitted by American authorities from entering the US though initially invited to read lections at a US theological university.

He came back to London and commented on his humiliation by the Americans: "I was forced to wait the entry permission usual for all Muslims for 8 hours sitting in a chair. Outside was the crowd eagor to congratulate me but I was separated from them. Finally the Americans told me I was not allowed to enter New York and I was expelled back to London".

The Pentagon admitted finally the arrests of 5 American citizens in Iraq "for their support of and cooperation with the Iraqi rebellion" Their arrests have been kept secrete up till now. The Iraqi government declined any comment.

14-07-21-07 - 2005

3 British soldiers were shot dead in an ambush at a British convoy in the British sector in South Iraq and 7 injured. The Dutch government which sent some 4,000 troops in the same sector-relativele calm one still keeps on silence on wether it will withdraw in September its contingent too together with the Italian contingent, mocked some British news papers. In Iskanderiya-85km south from Baghdad-a suicide bomber detonated his device at a police reqruitment station killing 20 people and injuring 31 others. In Musawiya-at a filling station near a Shiite mosque-a suicide bomber detonated his device under a petrol trucker killing 80 people and injuring 300 others. The huge blast destroyed or partly damaged many of the surrounding building sweeping at them tremendous tsunami of fire balls. Parents were seen throwing their children from the windows in futile attempt to rescue them while militants contunued their attck firing mortar shells at city square and the city market full with people in the early evening when the heat subsided.

In Baghdad several police stations were attacked in different city parts: the dead toll was 7 police men killed and 16 injured.

The Pentagon said :

"There's no sign of subsiding of violence in Iraq but terrorist violence fludded also neighbouring Turkey": Iraqi Kurdds travelled to the Turkish Egean resorts of Cesme & Kusa Dasi and detonated bombs in tourists` busses;20 people were injured in Cesme. In Kusa Dasi 6 people were killed in a mini-bus - 2 British tourists and one German woman. The British counsellar travelled from the capital Ankara to the scene of carnege in Kusa Dasi.

The British news paper Sunday Times discovered the MI5 dossier of the 4 bomber of the London tube. The police research protocol on the 25 years old Mohamed Khan and the MI5 police conclusion on him read: "He's good behaviour and poses no threat to public security?" The Sunday Times published this false report under the mocking & devastating title of "Terrorist is no public threat" (according to the police). There's no response neither from police nor from MI5 or MI6. Iraqi suicide fighter killed 8 recruits at a police recruitment center in Baghdad:he mingled with the crowd and than detonated his explosives belt. In Baquba American mini-bus came under fire and all 13 inmates were killed without mercy according to the holly book of Koraan. An independent British organization published a study already before the 07-07-2005 saying "the British invasion into Iraq has fueled up attacks against Britain and will threaten British & UK security". British Prime Minister Tony Blair & British Foreign Secretary Jack Straw said "they had had no knowledge of the report before and they don't agree with it afterwards because a lack of evidence". Their statements were welcomed by some Brits. Again in Iraq 2 Suni clerics suspended their membership into the constitution council aimed to draw up a new constitution because of the new suicide bomb attacks. Tony Blair & Jack Straw didn't comment on the scandal.

In Baghdad in the district of Mansur 2 Algerian diplomats were kidnapped the Algerian Ambassador and his deputy. Earlier the Egyptian Ambassador was kidnapped and subsequently killed.

In London 4 new explosions in the tube whirled the city into hell of panic. Later on police elucidated eloquently "these were no bombs but detonators". Because of the "strange smell police rushed into the tube with chemical protection suits". For many hours the tube was closed. One train station was closed too after an abandoned bag was discovered. The train drivers refused to enter the locomotives before discussion with the menagers. It was not clear iniatially how many people were killed or injured because police rejected any comments and asked eye witnesses to testify or to send MMS-pictures with their mobile phones to help police to discover or to arrest the suspects.

There were no killed and no injured-according to the police and the near by hospital;later on police arrested 2 suspects and special police forces stormed a hospital where one militant has been said to be in hiding but police issued no more details.

22 June-29 July 2005 Friday

Police in London shot dead a 29 years old Brasilian electrician because "he was looking different from the others, was relatively dark skin complexion and his clothes were different". This was the reason to shoot him dead without warning. After his execution it became clear "he had no explosives, no mobile phone and nothing which could be a link to terrorists, terror group or terror action", said a spokesman for the London police. The news papers accross Europe critisized sharply the Prime Minister Tony Blair for this step back from democracy saying "it is not acceptable to execute somebody in the street only because he's looking different from the others or he's running to catch the bus!" The Brasilian foreign minister met his British counterpart Jack Straw, critisized him sharply, demanded a full explanation and handed a protest of the Brasilian government to him. The Family of the killed man said "will prosecute the case and demand a compensation".

At the same time the terror groups hit in an entirely other place-in the Egyptian resort Sharm-el-Sheikh. They loaded a pick-up truck with explosives and drove it into a hotel packed with tourists killing 88 of them. Many others were seriously injured and died few days after the attack. The Egyptian government promised a full scale invesigation.

In Baghdad 8 police men were killed in 2 different car bomb attacks at police stations in two different parts of the city. The Bulgarian candidate for prime minister S. Stanishew promised to withdraw the Bulgarian troops from Iraq but he failed to form a cabinet after a whole month of political wrangling.

The Lybian government executed 11 for alleged different crimes. Some of them had spent already 10 years in jail. The US Defense Secretary Donald Rumsfeld visited Iraq and met the Iraqi Prime Minister Anwar Ibrahimi and the US commander in Iraq General Kassy. He said, it's quite possible for US troops to be withdrawn from Iraq after a 2-3 years` period. He did not meet any other commander from the American led coalition.

At the same time the Algerian foreign ministry admitted its kidnapped diplomats-the ambassador to Baghdad and his deputy-were killed by the guerrillas. They were kidnapped few days earlier and no ransom or political concessions were demanded for their lives.

16 Aug 2005

3 bomb attacks shattered the center of Baghdad after a police station was hit. Road side bombs and mortar fires attacked the ambulances rushing to the scene of disaster killing 40 and injuring 170 people in this new fashion of coordinated strategy of repulse. In the afternoon the Iraqi police announced the arrest of the 4 bombers after declaring initially the attacks "as suicide bomb attacks".

Independent journalists, NBC & CBS impeached also police of lying by discovering that the dead Brasilian man Menedesh was not a terrorist at all and had no suspicious behaviour as initially alleged by police. He had no sack and no luggage with himself, didn't jump at the tube springs' didn't run, was not warned by police-which was civil-didn't have a bulk jacket with explosives underneath as initially alleged and did not act suspiciously. Police simply shot him dead in cold blood without warning with 8 shots in his neck & one into his face according to the police "shoot to kill police tactic', explained human rights activist Rogger Craig to the CBS & NBS. Not a great difference to the Dutch police, he said.

25-26 August 2005

Attacks and explosions at one of the offices of the Suni cleric Moqtada al Sadr forced his militants to pay back with the same coin at Iraqi government targets. Above all the Suni position deteriorated after the Suni sector was cut off from he oil-rich provinces in the North & in the

South. US President bushed advised modestly the Iraqi people "to adopt the new constitution" which is rafting aroundalready for 3 weeks.

****

On 11 July 4 Taleban fighters managed to escape from American custody at the American air base Bagram near Kabul. 4 days later they joined the resurrected Taleban rebelion. The Pentagon rejected this statement and said "the search for the four continues "On 15 August 2005 17 Spanish soldiers died 70km northwest from Herat when their 2 helicopters were shot dawn. The Pentagon stated the helicopters colided in mid air but did not elucidate why. The Spanish defense minister contradicted saying both helicopters were shot down by the Afghan Taleban forces still undefeated. The Pentagon kept silence subsequently.

On 25 August 2005 the Uzbek government announced its decision to close the American air forces base at Herdan. It listed down 21 points to found its decision. The base was a key death factory during the war against the Afghan people in 2001-2002.

01 - 09 September 2005

While the daily US oil consumption amounted 20 mn barrels the price of the oil reached $70.75 a barrel.

One of the reasons was the huricane Katrina which devasted the Golf coast of the United States and stopped the oil production. The US Defense Secretary Donald Rumsfeld visited the flooded areas and sai "This is the biggest disaster in the history of the U.S.-much bigger than the 11th of September". The former US President Bill Clinton also visited the areas and required a "flood commission, similar to the 11th of September commission". His wife-Senator Hillary Clinton demanded almost the same. The area was ransacked further on by 2 more huricanes-Rita & Wilmar. Than the alphabetical list run out of names & it was decided to use Greek alphabet starting with <@> = "alpha". 2,500,000 homes remained with no electricity, said the governor of Florida Jeff Bush, Brother of George Bush.

Beyond Texas, Mississippi, Tennessi, Utah, Luisiana & Ohio 10 more states declared a state of emergency. The US State Department flew in 25,000 body bags but said "the number needed is much higher". Looters an gangsters attacked the survivors and hampered the rescue operations so that the police had to fire on them persistently. Police and National Guard arrested survivers and removed them forcibly in hand cuffs from the flooded areas into refugee camps. 40,000 more volunteers are estimated to be still needed. The US asked the UN for help but the air port of New Orleans is under water and no help could be flown in. It remained closed till 22 September 2005.

Under these cirrcumstances he Iraqi division of al Qaida posted immediately an Internet site stating "this was a divine holly wind and God had punished America for the war it unleashed in Iraq killing innocent civilians, women & children" and repeated the Saddam Hussein's statement from February 2001 when the American space shuttle Discovery collapsed and bursted out in flames killing all 7 astronauts on bord.

Saddam Hussein-than President of Iraq-said "God had punished America and all the world saw this". With his trial scheduled for 19 October 2005 Saddam Hussein is likely to make more similar statements, stressed the Al Qaida division of Iraq on its Internet site, posted on occasion of the American flood.

At the same time suicide bombers caused a stampede in Baghdad in which 650 people lost their lives. In Tal Afar 70 rebels were killed but they menaged to shot down an American helicopter gun ship. In Basra 70 Iraqi police officers were killed when a suicide driver rammed his car into a cafe visited by Iraqi police men.

In another attack in Basra 4 British & 2 American soldiers were killed. So only now we learnt that there are also American troops in the Basra sector, not only British & Dutch as previously deliberated. One British soldier was killed additionally and 4 other injured when they patrol car hit a road side bomb also in Basra. So the number of the British soldiers killed this week reached 5- a gloom futuristic prognosis at a price.

The Riverhead Books published a new book on Iraq written by an American soldier who spent a wholle year in Iraq and put down his memories, emotions and impressions.

12 September 2005

The Israeli troops left the Gaza strip they've occupied for 38 years. For the first time in 38 years the media spit out the words "occupation" & "occupiers" we'd never heard before. The Iraqi President Ibrahim al Jafari visited the liberated city of Tal Afar and praised the Iraqi & American troops for "their joint exploit & heroism in liberating the city from rebels". In fact the rebels were only their own sisters & brothersengulfed into a long-standing civil war with a remarkable prolongation. Why not-the Holly Bible has its root and was born exactly here in this areas quite before the times it describes.

The Iraqi leader Jelal Talebani met President Bush in Washington. After menaging the flood crisis in New Orleans President Bush stated "Iraq must menage its crisis with the rebels by an entirely new approach", "the US will meet the enemies of Iraq by a strong arm", "there is no time table to withdraw the American troops from Iraq" (what about the other allies?) aand "he'll take fool responsibility bout the the victims & the blunders round the flood in advance & afterwards". All the world foolly believed to him.

The British Chancellor of the Exchequer Bachelor Gorden Brown asked the world to "reduce the oil prices rocketing to the skies". And he asked the world to "increase the oil output to meet the demands", as he put it long before the begin of the winter period while a big strike is already been growing in Britain. He tried to avert it- why not - but already on Wednesday the British started to queue up at petrol stations and to pile up oil reserves. At 14 SEPT a long series of 10 huge bomb explosions shattered Iraqi Capital Baghdad killing 200 people and injuring 280 others. The first explosion hit workers at a square queueing up in a Shiite square for wages in the early morning hours. 118 lost their lives in a tremendous explosion of 500 kg explosives. 9 other mighty explosions followed turning up Baghdad into living hell of inferno, chaos & carnage. The malicious day began at night when a single sniper mowed down 17 people already at night. The Iraqi al Qaida-a group never heard of under Saddam Hussein-stated at its Internet site "It's our al Qaida retaliation for the Tal Afar slaughter of American victims". As a matter of memory the American war on al Qaida started in 2001 and drifted from Afghanistan to Iraq but in fact overwhelmed the world for American needs & US oil demands. The American spokesman in Iraq collonnel Dan Bryan replyed "This is a vain attempt of remaining terrorists to gain upper hand in the face of the American advances in Iraq & in the face of the forthcoming Iraqi consti tution due to be voted on on 15ᵗʰ of October ": 4 days before the trial of the former President Saddam Hussein, who never opposed America by military means and never warfared against America during his time of 25 years in presidential office.

At the opening session of the UN the Iraqi leader Talebani said "the world must do more for Iraq" & "the (US?) dictatorship for Iraq must end". He found no responseafront the oil crisis burning red currently and in the future-the main reason for the 2ⁿᵈ war against the Arabs for oil, big money & big humiliation.

The bomb attacks in Iraq increased reaching a new peak. On 15ᵗʰ SEPT in Dura in South Baghdad suicide car driver detonated his bombs at police point killing 21 cops injuring much more others. When special forces circled that area they got attacked again by the patriots their snipers scything around Islam. In Kirkuk & Falluja the road side bombs of the resistense met their targets & their American targets met their faith and their cowboy destiny as their oath of alleageance obliged them to meet. And on Sunday the MP Faris Hussein was shot dead in the center of Baghdad together with his body guard while another MP was injured by a single gun man.

19-25 September 2005

While the rebels rammed a camicaze car into American diplomatic convoy killing 4 the British down in Basra destroyed the wall of an Iraqi police station to release two British soldiers from an Iraqi police station. Initially they were arrested for walking & spying around in civil Arab clothes with all amounts of weapons. After their arrest the Iraqi interior minister ordered their release but they were conveyed to a local militia station instead. So the Brits had no choice but to break the wall of the station & to release their comrades. The Iraqis launched an investigation into the whole matter lavishly revived by the British Press on Monday. & Tuesday. On Wednesday the Iraqi prime minister Ibrahim al Jafari was summoned to London to explain the matter. At same time some 200 angry people demonstrated at the police head quarters in

Basra demanding the resignation of the chief of police. The British Defense Secretary John Reed stressed,

"Brits will not simply cut & go despite the fact many Iraqi police cooperate closely with the insurgents". In fact the Iranian newspaper Idilive noticed "the Brits were undercovered soldiers with explosives & weapons on a terrorist action to get blamed on the Iraqis-militias & insurgents. Iran is strong enough to warn the Brits to withdraw from Basra & South Iraq where Iran has strong influensce & strong support among the population. Marking the 25th anniversary from the begin of the notorious Iran-Iraq-war, remembering all the victims from the both sides Iran does advise all foreign troops to withdraw from Iraq in order to save demo cracy, freedom, stability, dignity & good neighbourhood", the paper read for the mankind.

The Iraqi Mayor of Basra rejected any cooperation or support with the Brits, said CNN. The Iraqi judge Raged al Musabr issued an arrest warrant for the two Brits in connection with the murder of one Iraqi civilian and the injury of a police man on Monday, when the two undercovered soldiers opened fire and were detained but later on forcibly freed by their collegues. The British authorities said "the arrest warrant lacks any legal base" and "the British instructors in Iraq train police men which later cooperate with the extremists". In a Sunday anti-war demonstration in London the British Prime Minister Tony Blair stressed again "the British forces will stay in Iraq as long as needed". Meanwhile in Baghdad the forces of Moqtad al Sadr attacked the American forces killing 8 soldiers. In a car bomb explosion 5 additional troops were killed.

Meanwhile in Texas began the 2nd trial against the prison guard Lindsey England accused of prisoners' abuse at the notorious Abu Ghraib prison near Baghdad. Her husband sergeant Crage received already his sentence of 10 years and started serving them. So many expected that England will be sentenced only to 5 years in jail. Her judge is the German Doctor Pohl.

The US decreased their oil production again ahead the expected new hurricane Rita in the Mexican golf which rapidly gained magnitude < 4 > equal to 240kmh-the same magnitude which gained also hurricane Katrina 3 weeks ago. The huricane seems to approach the Texas East coast where Americans evacuate their own people aong overall panic. This shot up oil prices again in the skies. The national Nasa center in Huston was evacuated too-including the New Orleans' refugees fleeing from Katrina. "Living on the brink became a part of the American culture", commented an American judge. The huricane hit Texas & Luisiana and in New Orleans the water levels started to rise again so that the American troops had to patrol the streets only on boots. The evacuees ran short of food, water & fuel and stranded on roads coasing huge traffic jams in which some 24 people lost already their lives. 50 oil rafineries were closed in Texas protective ly while the previous huricane Katrina destroyed 14 rafineries from the very beginning. Rita started with destroying 14 electrical tarffoposts.

27-09-2005

In The Hague Dutch police started trial against the independent journalist Emil Tzolov but in Iraq only one bullet went off & murdered Abu al Jahari known as Abu al Assam-allegedly number 2 of the Iraqi al Qaida. "Al Qaida nr.1 Al Zarqawi waits for his bullet too", read some intimidations to follow. What're the nick names of Emperor Forrest or King La Toya Blur in dirthy American anecdotes? The murder of Abu al Jahary in his Baghdad flat after a single shot "followed after a public tip-off" awarded by sorded $700 equal to 100 liters of native Iraqi gasoline. The next day a female suicide bomber detonated her device at an army reqruit station in Tal Afar killing 18 candidate-killers of the sort above. This is the first lady-attack in Iraq. Her blown-up head was delivered to a police station in a plastic bag by Iraqis not by Americans;the bomber. Her name was not revealed. In Tehran a petrol bomb was thrown at the British embassy as a protest against escalation.

In Baghdad the brother of the interior minister was shot dead while driving his car through a Shiite area. The Shiite kept on surpressing continuosly the Suni insurgence. In al Sadr in al Anbari province in western Iraq the Americans started a great offensive against the Sunis. This city is only 12km away from the Syrian border and is strongly believed to be a main point for shipping weapons and personel for the insurgents but no prisoners of war as the Americans put it.

After the Americans killed 12 people the population fled away afront the approaching American avelanche-some 1,000 marines & helicopters said American correspondent Jennifer Ekelstone. Their number turned to be 2,500 in the week to follow.

03-10 October 2005

The Iraqi oil minister Ibrahim bar al Olum and his body-guards were killed when a suicide bomber hit his convoy in Baghdad. Later on the news was he'd survived his body guards. A proposal was made to prosecute all insurgency attacks as war crimes. Well, all insurgency attackers were suicide bombers so they're dead by this proposal. How to trial them-in heaven as they desired to fly onto or into the hell of war, war crimes and petrol chaos America flunged our world in?? The war crime tribunal in The Hague refused-as usual-to comment on the issue but many commentators noted "Carla del Ponte is not the EU"&

Carla del Ponte is not any EU-state even". Carla del Ponte praised highly the Croatian position on Monday after she has been critisizing Croatia vehemently on Friday. Croatia saved its comments & critics to Carla del Ponte. One of the reasons is that the Muslim country of Turkey is been applying this weekend all day & all night for its EU membership. The birth growing rate of Turkey is very high-over 170,000 children a year based partly on Turkish yeni chari poilicy;so with 40% population under 22 Turkey is expected to become the most populous EU-nation in 2020 overgrowing Germany & France, the Brits rejoyced with delight.

"With no Turks EU will become a solitude Christian club", Turkey countered.

The Iraqi foreign ministry apologized to Saudi Arabia for his remark "Saudi Arabia is very bad-worse even than a camel". Bayan al Jawar-a pro-American made his remark unprovoked. My persoannel opinion is that a camel is a very nice, very tamed animal better than any other definitely better than any american. But nevertheless the pro-american minister made his anti-american remark after all.

After the attack against the oil minister Ibrahim bar al Olum (not Olsun) he was said to have survived it unlike his body guards. The attack came only 12 days ahead the Iraqi referendum for constitution which is largely expected to vote "no" by 2 thirds of the voters-it liked the European constitution vote which shattered on the "no"-vote of the Dutch voters in June 2005 against the constitution against all govern mental agitations & leaflets to the voters which is actually forbidden all over the world not in Holland. The Iraqi government proposed a new scheme to block the expected Suni "no" vote on 15 October which additionally angered the Suni voters. The UN critisized the Iraqi governmental vote practice.

In al Anbari province the Americans launched the massive River Gate military operation meant to overwhelm even the previos Iron Fist & Sword operation engaging 2,500 marines, Iraqi troops & traitors against an enemy who'd fled already that area long before the American assault. No military success was reported bilaterally.

The Iranian foreign minister Manousheer Moutaki visited Saudi Arabia to smooth down some disputed issues;the Saudi government accuses Iran for interfering into the Iraqi affairs mostly by using its influence over the Iraqi Shiite majority. The British accused Iran too of smuggling sophisticated weapons into Iraq which killed 8 British soldiers in Basra this summer. But Iran denied the allegations. Nevertheless the Brits arrested additionally 12 more Iraqis in Basra and interrogated them aggressively; among them were also army & police officers.

Palestinian officials incl. Nabil Shaath published interview with President George W. Bush in which he admitted that "God had spoken to him and advised him to start the Afghan war, the Iraqi war and than to settle the Palestinian issue", BBC said at 10.04 GMT on 07-10-2005. Many Arab news papers incl. the London based alQuds al Arabi published the Bush interview with the remark "if a normal man makes such a remark he will be arrested and than put into a lunatic asylum; such a remark could be made only by man who is not mentally sound":www.alquds.co.uk

White House spokesmen incl. Scott McClellan dismissed the "Palestinian claims as baseless, roumours & allegation" but more details are expected next week, BBC vowed. The Americans tried to white wash the scandal but the core of the fact is that already during the Afghan war his underaged niece Noelle Bush-than 20-was arrested & charged when tried to get the psychopharmaca Xanax psychoparmacum-an anti-anxiety drug-on a false receipt in a local Florida chemistry. The exact day was 29 January 2002. Afterwards there were no further reports on her court trial. Than the Bush's "regreted the case" as "a very serious one", they put it.

To play down the scandal the Bush's focused on the bird flue vaccine and urged the world in a special conference "to produce urgently a vaccine against the bird flue in Asia"-after some

36 months of delay ; than all of the sudden the Pentagon claimed "it intersepted the letter of al Qaida activist al Zahari to Jordanian militant al Zarqawi with instructions how to fight further in Iraq & than to export the fight to neighbouring countries" as if the USA's not exporting it already world wide-at least not by the oil price.

Scott Ritter gave extensive interview to the BBC. Speaking to Carry Gracy he said "President Bush knew pretty well Saddam had no weapons of mass destruction, the Iraqi elections were falsified and the war in Iraq is unwinable, it can even escalate further". He stressed the role of the CIA & the American Embassy in Iraq for buying votes against the Suni and several million dollars changed hands in this campaign. He explained also the role of the CIA in organizing the coup attempt against Saddam Hussein in 1996 and critisized bitterly the corruption within the US government. Scott Ritter was chief weapon inspector for Iraq but resigned in 1999 and became outspoken critic of president Bush and his blood sheds in Iraq. The full text & sound of his interview was broadcasted world wide.

The Abu Musab al Zarqawi group started a recruiting internet page & a weekly web site. The recruitment page asks for volunteers with English and Arabic to advertise and to take photos & videos of suicide bomb attacks against western targets. It can & will communicate also with Islamic organizations & news papers though privately. In Karam & in Falluja road side bombs killed 6 American soldiers. The Bulgarians said they will pull off their troops from Iraq by 14 December 2005 but the Americans countered them by saying "they cannot provide any proper convoy to them to pull out". The Grand Ayatollah of Iraq Ali al Sistani summoned all Iraqi clerics not to support any candidate in the forthcoming elections "otherwise he'll risk to lose his support".

10-17 October 2005

The family of John Charles de Menazes arrived from Brasil in London to investigate the death of their son and brother. Mr. de Manazes was shot deat by mistake because "he was looking suspiciously to the police" But it became clear he was not running away, but was apprehended at at atrain waggon and there shot dead executionary style. The cost for the travel of his family were paid by the British police.

In Tal Afar in northern Iraq near the Syrian border a car bomb went off at a busy market place killing 35 people. In Baghdad a car bomb kill 4 people. Later on again in Baghdad 6 Iraqi soldiers were shot dead in separate attacks. The Saudi King Fahid said "he will do everything possible to destroy al Qaida, because al was a net work of devil", he vowed. But one day before the referrendum heavy bomb explosions shattered the headquarters of the Suni Islamic Party in Baghdad and in Falluja killing 8 people. The Sunis had decided to vote against the referrendum. The day of the referrendum-Saturday, 15 October-heavy gun fire was heard in Ramadi. The next day 3 rockets hit different targets in the Green Zone in Baghdad. On other spots 6 Americans were killed. The result of the constitution referrendum remained unclear and Condoleeza Rice didn't comment on it: after a private lunch with Tony Blair in London she flew back to Washington without any comment. The referendum result will be clear a week later but UN Secretary General Kofi Annan praised it already now.

The British presented to Iran samples of explosives used by Iran to kill British in Iraq, they claimed. Iran dis missed their claim with the words "..during the 8 years war there remained many Iranian weapons in Iraq and many Iraqi weapons in Iran!"

The same referendum night the US military killed 71 insurgents near Ramadi in 2 separate attacks. The first air plane attack killed 20 people "gathering to plant a new road side bomb on the place of a previous bomb which killed 7 Americans few days earlier". The second air craft attack was few miles away "obliterating 51 insurgents". And this was a week end, a referendum day! Civil doctors & Iraqi police said "this were at least 51 civil citizewns, not a single militant". In Germany in the struggle against terrorism the German interior minister Otto Schilly changed the color of the police cars from white-green to blue-green, the international color, he put it.

18-23 October 2005

The Iraqi special supervisor of the referrendum Adel Alami said to BBC "the irregularities amounted to a vote fraude". In Baghdad started the trial against Saddam Hussein and 7 of his former collegues. Saddam refused to tell the court his name and his profession saying "you're Iraqi, you know my name, you know I am President of Iraq & you know that your court has no legitimacy". Without standing up from the dock Saddam Hussein pleaded calmly "not guilty" and refused to cooperate further with the court. Cooperate in which direction? Looking pale but absolutely calm, serving further to his nation against the Americans, more black-bearded than grey he had brisk & commanding style of manners & gestures, said BBC diplomatic correspondent James Reynoulds "from the court well", as he put it.

Saddam's microphones were cut so the journalists couldn't understand very clearly what he's saying. Saddam is accused of the mass execution of 140 Shiite men after the failed assassination attempt on him in 1982. Later on the trial was ajurned for 28 November. Many Arabs feel his trial as a vindication for his defiance to America, some journalists dared to say under the muzzle. Saddam's trial has been watched by some 100,000,000 all over the world and they said "this was a show trial, the strings were pulled behind by the occupiers of the Arab world". Many other expressions were censorshipped.

Saddam repeated many times befor retreatring to the the dock that the court was incompetent & illigimate, BBC correspondent Jim Simpson said on air in the mess of chaos this empty day. Saddam never said the words "guilty" or "mercy"-neither to the Court, nor to God, nor to the Press, nor to the oil-empty, oil-greedy West, Iraq was been serving to. This is the begining of a very long winter. Finally Saddam's co-defense lawyer was arrested (=apprehended) "by armed men", as the American Iraqis put it. Saddam's lawyer Abdul al Khalami said to BBC "no body is safe in Saddam's trial-not the prosecution witnesses, not the defense witnesses, not the defense lawyers, not even me!" He put the vi ctims of the 2 years'civil war to 250,000 Iraqis. The trial was ajurned to 28 November 2005:this time Saddam Hussein will have spenfd in jail as before. Obviously not for his own glory.

The Irish journalist Ronnie Carol (not o'Carol) from The Guardian was released from prison & left Iraq: "These were Iraqi police in Iraqi police uniforms-either stolen or genuine, the Iraqi police is infiltrated by Suni militants, by Iraqi insurgents who waved away the results of the referendum waiting for the new parliamentary elections in December 2005", Ronny Carol said before leaving Iraq.

24-30 October 2005

3 heavy truck bomb explosions hit Baghdad's hotels Palestine & Sheraton exactly the area where most foreign journalists & contractors live killing 12 of them. In Musaib a single gun man shot dead 12 contract workers when returning from work.

2 Iraqi Suni dominated provinces had voted with "NO" against the recent referendum. Now remains the 3rd province of Ninewa to say "NO" to invalidate the vote. It said it but could not gain the 66% majority needed so the referendum for new constitution was valid and opened the way for new parliamentary elections in December 2005.

The Russian foreign minister Sergey Lawrow said "the UN oil-for-food-papers were false-many signatures of different officials were faked".

~~~~~~~~~~~~~~~~~~~~~

The special US prosecutor Fitzgerald accused the White House & especially the presidential advisor Carl Rove and the White House chief of staffLouis Scubby Libbie of deliberately betraying the name of the acting CIA agent Vallory Plame-wife of the former US Ambassador Joe Williams who in 2003 contradicted the White House & personally President Bush "alleged findings of uranium purchase from Nigeria for the Iraqi nuclear weapons of mass destruction program"-a futile lie to the whole world in more than 11,000 pages. In revenge his wife's name was given out.

The scandal may demand finally the resignation of president George W. Bush, said BBC on Monday.

Other experts demanded the penalty for treason & for misleading the nation into war.

BBC itself announced plans to to set up a 12 hours television channel in Arabic language for the Middle East by March 2007. To offset the costs it will cut off 8 of 12 radio channels-66%-but oil rich education poor Romania and tungsten rich Thailand were excluded from the Foreign Office' list. More over in Thailand Muslim militants attacked 20 government targets in one week and plundered over 1,000 guns so that it may remain further focus of clashes.

~~~~~~~~~~~~~~~~~~~~~

In 3 car bomb explosions at the security ministry and at a car convoy in Suleymaniya 19 people died. The senior Kurdish official Mula Bhakti survived the attacks which initially aimed at him. The president Jalal Talebani who is from the ruling PUK-party was also in the area on an extended visit but remained unhurt.

Suleymaniya was considered for a pretty calm place and economy there was been thriving.

The RF - chip emits impulses, so that they could be read from distance like bar code - the core of the bugging both for phones & computers. RF means radio frequency. Nothing can be to getém stopped.

In Baquba 26 people died in a car bomb attack aimed at the American puppit governmet, 66 were injured in the American pleasure; in New Delhi the killed amounted to 99 while the injured were over 200: again a pleasure-for the glory of America not the author of this book.

01-11-2005

Despite the heavy 6 American marines losses in Baghdad in one nicht President Bush spoke of global warming.

****

12 Sept 2005

The American forces released the captured Taleban Ambassador to Pakistan Abdul Salam Zaif from the Guantanamo base prison. Mr. Zaif spent 4 years in American custody without charges after he's unlawfully arrested at the Afghan Embassy in Islamabad in October 2001. Mr. Zaif is expected to arrive somewhere in the world and to get interviewed there. He's not expected to flee or whisper about the conditions of detention but to stress that the American war against the Afghan people and against the Arab world had failed: "Neither Osama ben Laden nor Mula Omar were arrested after such an expensive war", he's expected to say "nor the so called "world" became a safer place to war fare there. The Brother of Osama ben Laden even registered a new trade company in Swiss, named Islam abin Laden". All this at the background of the American intimidation to use nuclear weapons against terrorists. Neither US Defense Secretary Donald Rumsfeld nor President Bush signed it yet.

The Afghan President Hamed Kharzai stated in a BBC-interview "America must review revise its policy in "the US war against terrorism"". Shortly before his interview a mighty bomb explosion shattered Kandehar killing 2 American soldiers while on a patrol. Bush & the White House gave no reply. Later on President Bush flew back to Washington to meet the Iraqi leader Jelal Talebani for an afternoon.

At the opening session of the UN Talebani said "the world must do more for Iraq" & "the (US?) dictator ship for Iraq must end". He found no response in the face of the burning oil crisis.

18 September 2005 Sunday

The Afghan elections went well under way being supervised by 30,000 Afghan troops and 41,000 American troops. Their result was : 3 bomb explosions in Pakistan killing 6 people.

25-30 September 2005

An American Chinouk helicopter came down in Southern Afghanistan killing all 5 soldiers on board. The Taleban said, they have shot down the helicopter. In Bali & in Kuta in Indonesia a spade of bomb attacks shattered the pleasure of this idyllic resort killing 25 & injuring 60 tourists. The police distributed in the news papers photos and on television broadcastings the cut heads of the suspected suicide bombers and than asked the public-not paid by police-to recognize them in order to get a clue to the organizers and to the back-uppers-all allegedly from Jemaah Islamiya, as repeated already many times though in private.

08 October 2005 09.45

A disatrous earth quake shattered Afghanistan, Pakistan, Kashmir & India killing thousands of people : "the earth kept rocking for 6 long minutes", eyewitnesses said ; "an unprecedented quake since centuries with tremendous destructive power", geologist commented the tragedy. The quake was 7.7 on the Richter schale with epycenter in Kashmir where the killed were 18,000 people already in the first day. In Muzafar abad 11,000 people died, in Tandar-3,500. On the 4th day the Pakistani government declared the number of the dead as high as 35,000 ;the number of refugees-between 427,000 - 1,000,000.

Heavy rains & mud slides hampered the rescue operation. The nightly temperatures fall to minus 5 degrees Celsius in the mountains; so the final number of the death by the week rose to 40,000 in Kashmir & to 55,000 in Pakistan.15,000 villages were destryed. Exactly one week later another earth quake rocked Tokyo; it measured 5.1 on the Richter scale. Specialists said "the quakes were direct results of the heavy US-bombardment of these areas by the Americans in the Afghan war 2001-2002"

The Tajik government expelled the Americans from their Tajik air bases. But the US manged to retain their Uzbek base Manzes "after tough negotiations of the Uzbeks with doctor Condoleeza Rice".

2 rockets exploded in Kabul shortly before the visit of the US secretary of state Condoleeza Rice there;one hit the Canadian Embassy, the other one the building of the Afghani Intelligence office. Afterwards Condo leeza Rice-a new backed doctor-cut short her visit to Afghanistan and flew to Paris for meetings with EU-leaders and than to London for a private lunch with the British Prime Minister Tony Blair.

19-10-2005

The American defense secretary Donald Rumsfeld visited China and more specially the strategic missile center. He is the first American leader to do so.

The Australian television channel SBS broadcasted a video footage showing American soldiers burning Taleban combatants. On another film they were shown beating & mocking at local villagers, on a 3rd film-using dioxin to smoke Taleban out their hidings. The Australina journalist Martincek was at the same time a cameraman, he was embedded into an American military unit for some time. The US Army said it will launch a criminal investigation into the alleged abuses of human dignity.

****

Jennifer Ekelstone-American correspondent in Iraq during the Anbari invasion in October 2005

Bayan al Jawar-Iraqi deputy foreign minister: "The Saudi's are worse than any camel", he said

Sadr-Iraqi city in the western al Anbari province heavily destroyed by american raids against Syria.

Ibrahim bar al Olum-Iraqi oil minister, survived assassination attempt on 03-10-2005.

EU-abreviation for the European Union not unity

WW2- abbreviation for the world war two

Abdul Akbar Bashir-Jemaah Islamiya leader, jailed for 2 years for his views unlike G. Bush who was not Iron Fist - splended American military operation against Iraqi Sunis in September 2005

Sword-splended American military operation against Iraqi Sunis in 2005

River Gate-American operation against Iraqi Sunis in October 2005 close to the Syrian peace border

Scott Ritter-US weapon inspector in Iraq;resigned 1999;critisized bitterly "the Bush unwinable Iraq war"

Scott McClellan-spokesman for President George W. Bush

ahram.daily@ahram.org.eg - an Arabic newspaper

www.alquds.co.uk - an Arabic London based bilinguial news paper

John Charles de Manazes-Brasilian student shot dead by mistake by British police in July 2005

Tal Afar-city at the Iraqi-Syrian border where many fierce battles took place

Manzes-US air base in Uzbekistan "retained after tough negotiations with the Uzbeks" in October 2005

Raggath Hussein-the eldest daughter of president Saddam Hussein

Roy Carol-Irish journalisof The Guardian, kidnapped by Iraqi police in October 2005, than released

250,000-the number of the Iraqis killed by October 2005, so BBC

Martinczek-Australian journalist, filmed for CBC-TV the US atrocities in Afghanistan in 2005

death sentences-in the USA comes into force only after presidential signature

Abdul al Khalami-the lawyer of Saddam Hussein, worked for free, interviewd by BBC on 22-10-2005

Ninewa-Suni dominated province, voted "NO" against George Bush, but failed to produce 66% majority

01-11-2005

Despite the heavy loss of 6 American marines in Baghdad only in one night President Bush spoke of global warming. One year after his re-election he faced severe criticism of his policy "which is decided in Baghdad and not in the rural villages of America". Over 51% of the people consider the war in Iraq "for a mistake", said Clair Boldoson in BBC. At the same time the anti-war protests in Paris kept on raging for a whole week after police killed 2 teenagers aged 14 & 18. The rioting youth set afire 2900 cars, 27busses in a depot, 30 hotels, plundered over 1,000 shops, postoffices, schools, trew stones, bottles, bricks, fired petrol bombs, life amunition, attacked police, spread the riot up to the cities of Dijon, Buche de Rhone, Rouen, Nice, Adrenne, Marceille, Toullouse, Strasbourg and Lille ; Lille is only 30km away from Belgium ;similar to the scenes in the British Birmingham riots whole last week. "These riots vented the problems of the past 30 years", said the French interrior minister Nicolas Sarkuzy, after calling the rioters "scum" and using street language among calls for his resignation. His response was "More arrests! More arrests-this is the key!"

Late on Sunday night the French President Chirac said "the priotity is to restore order".

A British court marshall acquitted 7 British soldiers in Iraq for assaulting, beating & killing an 18-ager Iraqi 2 years earlier-Naddam Abdullah. The judge said, "the evidences were too vague, week & contradicting". In A British civil court revoked a court decision on "the suicide of 4 soldiers:it was a clear murder", said Gill Fidgeon & Rob Watson from the BBC, naming no reasons. In Hasayba-12km from the Syrian border the Americans started freshs attack against the insurgents killing 250 local people. The junkies called the operation "Steel Curtain", the Arabs- Fallujah Sunrise. Fallujah became the symbol of the all-arab resistence against americans in 2004 and now it will become the name of my book against American blood sheds all over the worlds.

Major General Jimmy Dutton told the public that "new technology of making bombs & bombs equipments entered Iraq from Iran, but's not sure if the Iranian leaders knew about the boundary transfer", while police imposed curfue for a pleasure.

In Mar del Plata in Argentina opened the 44th American Senate with demonstrators such as Hugo Chaves & Diego Maradonna protesting against the USA. The Venezuela president Hugo

Chaves called bluntly the American war in Iraq "a terrorist war, not a mistake". The Paraguayan president Leylla Rashida said "the contradiction between Bush & Chaves should not dominate the meeting".

An unannounced German lawyer used the France created situation to issue his long time prepared book "We love Hitler and why?!". His name was not announced for a frog.

All the surprise the the the Irqai laweyr of Sadddam Hussein was shot dead by a precises American sniper: Abdul al Zubaidy lost his life-but not his family-after a shot into his international heart. When's my turn?? Some pronounced his name as al Zubawi, while 3 suicide bombers made a fire work at Aman's luxurous hotels in Jordan killing 55 & injuring 120 people, whiled the killed in Baghdad were 3 and in Tikriti-6 Ameri can merceneries. The Jordanian police paraded one of the suicider-her explosive belt didn't go off and she was arrested and interrogated. The Jordanian Al Haleli tribal clan impeached Abul al Zarqawi and denoun ced, saying it cuts all familly relations to him & pledged oath of alleagence to the Jordanian King Abdulhah 2. Mass riots followed. Few days on a bomb hit Baghdad killilling 8 merceneries in Hanekenim in northern Iraq bordering Iraq & Turkey the killed were 68 plus the injured heroes of America.

Washington demanded wisely the Syrian cooperation for an assassination a whole year earlier. In the 1960ies American President Kennedy was shot dead by a sniper and the "sniper was shot dead by policemen but the whole story loved getting yet another nuance of non-investigation"

Saddam Hussein's NR.2, his deputy Ibrahim al Alduri, leader of Baath and of the post Saddam insurgen ce was finally shot dead-but in Iraq, not in Syria-as the Americans kept on asserting he's hiding in. What to say 'bout my hiding place?! The American price on his head was single 10,000,000 USD with an unclear origin of shame. Nothing was said on his burrial & his resting place as usual; probably from price on his head : "He was not killed in a battle, he simply died but not in Syria wherer he was thought to be hiding but in Iraq. Any way his death is a very good news for Iraq", said the Iraqi president Jalal Talebani. In fact his statement came only few hours after rumours that AL Zarqawi was shot dead in a skirmish. His head or body was not paraded but DNA-tests were taken- he knows his DNA as good as George Bush does know his own DNA legend as a well. Only a day later US marines stormed the building of the Shiite hold ministry of foreign affairs in whose undergrounds 174 Sunis were imprisoned and tortured: "The torture of Sunis by our Shiite forces is quite a general but useful praxis", admitted the leader of the Shiite party Traik al 'Hashami. The Sunis called for an international investigation for the glory of the UN.

Finally it became clear, the illegal prison was run by the Iraqi interrior ministry and the heads cut there among the tortures & dehumiliations were for his account. The Pentagon announced, it will stop run the illegal prison but met fierce resistance from the Iraqi interrior ministry. The Iraqi President Jalal Talebani visited Teheran and asked Iran for help to stop the insurgents. Theran in turn promised to do so but asked him for a final term to get foreign troops get withdrawn from Iraq. The British said the start of the British troops withdrawal will begin in 2007 and a former British defense minister revealed there were secrete talks between Tony

Blair and George Bush to bombard the Arabic television station al Jezeera. Tony Blair denied any knowledge of such talks, but journalist Cohen McGeyern sayd "it was an ill joke"-as ill as many others

The British advised the Bulgarians to withdraw their 3,700 troops-which is already decided-but to replace them by a new contingent of 1,200 which will secure the refugee camp of Saliya 70km north-east from Baghdad. Britain expulsed 15 Iraqi refugees and asylum seekers back to Iraq because "it was safe now for the to live there".

In Mahmudiya a car bomb explosion killed 4 Americans, 6 Iraqi soldiers and 30 civilians; the suicide bomber rammed his explosives-packed car into a military convoy.

In Kirkut a suicide fighter killed 18 American soldiers: he inscened a small attack & than drew up marines to heaven. Abul al Havi admitted-after been tortured to death by Saudi forces-he's plotting to ass assinate president Bush. Al of the sudden his trial was delayd till 02 February 2006

In the Turkish province of Hakari bordering Iran & Iraq police exploded a bomb in a book store to kill a Kurdish militant and than shot round vehemently at the crowds... Turkish police is repeatedly accused of breeding strong gendarmery divisions to kill Kurds extrajudicially.

In Baghdad 4 Canadian humanitarian worker an 7 Iranian pilgrims were kidnapped, 4 British killed by gun men in an attack on their mini-bus but the Iraqi President Jalal Talebani decided to dennounce the former prime minister Ayad Allawi "for speaking nonsense that under Saddam was safer". Few days later on he visited the Imam Ali Shrine in Najaf to speak for the consolidation of the nation but the Suni fighters of the militant Moqtada al Sadr organized an attempt on his life and some of his body guards were badly injured.

Alawi narrowly avoided certain deathe by running away when Moqtad al Sadr aproached him with swords and gun fire-the same style of assassination of another Shiite cleric-Nasab Najib al Ahuy in April 2004.

The US Army started a new military offensive called "Iron Hammer" against the insurgents in Hit & Ramadi President Bush said in a speech "The USA will not run away from several car bombers until I am commander in chief!" In Belgium and in France police arrested several potential al Qaida reqruits ready to join the Iraqi insurgents. But in Fallujah the Americanscame under fire while on patrol and 10 marines lost their lives by Suni gunmen. North West from Baghdad Iraqi soldiers came under fire and 19 of them were killed. Initially their convoy was attacked by road side bomb. After wards the insurgents opened fire on the fleeing soldiers and 19 of them were killed.

02-11-2005

The Washington Post reported that CIA runs since 2001 series of secrete prisons abroad mostly in "friendly countries" such as Holland, Thailand, Afghanistan, former East Block countries-such as hungry Romania, corrupt Bulgaria etc... There suspected al Qaida detainees were allegedly interrogated without any chance to confront their cases & withouth any human rights. By this "method" the prisoners are deprived of normal judicial procedures in courts. Red Cross speaker Antonella Lothari demanded Red Cross' imme diate access to all undisclosed prisons in 8 "friendly countries". Dr. Rice praised this praxis known as

< RENDITION >:

prisoners's transfer into different countries for interrogations using the local law;but she rejected any claim of torture of prisoner, detainees and "illegal combatants": "Everything was in the frame of the international law, we use only lawful means in the battle against international terrorists in the strugle to defeat them fully & entirely, the CIA has not used third contries, their airspaces, their air fields, their prisons for interrogation & everything is according the old rules of war", boasted Dr. Rice to the BBC diplomatic correspondent John athan Marcus on 05 December 2005. In fact CIA used massively chemicals & narcotics to destabalize'm mentally & to declare'm insane: "to make them soft & dizzy ":it is an old Dutch praxis widely used in Holland with its large prisons' network despite the country's budget deficiency. But Condoleeza Rice-doctor of law- denied any torture in CIA-prisons as "a lie; <RENDITION> was used in the case of Karlos-The Jackal; more over many of these fighter are statless". In fact CIA asked Germany to keep quite over <RENDITION> of a captured German fighter and Germany did in breach of the Geneva-convention on prisoners & jails. Shortly after her statement she flew to Holland to discuss the <RENDITION> issue with Dutch officials. Holland runs a dense prison network despite its huge budget deficiency.

05-15 December 2005

In the trial of Saddam Hussein his defese lawyers walked out of court room to protest. His main defense lawyer is Clark Ramadi-former US attorney general. The first witness Ahmed Mohamed gave confused rambling 40 minutes' evidences on the Dujail mass killings of Kurds back in 1985 interrupted frequently by Saaddam's half-brother Barzan al Tikriti until his full confusion. In his 15-minutes' speech Saddam dominated the court & declared angrily "I am not afraid of execution-if you want my neck-here you are! Important is not Saddam but Iraq's glory in this political show-trial! Long live Iraq! Down with the American dictators!", shouted Saddam dominating the court in whose legality he doubted. After these words the defense lawyers left the court in protest. Saddam himself state "he was tortured & beaten by the Americans in their rough justice".

In Baghdad a suicide bomber detonated his explosive belt in a full-packed bus bound to Mosul killing 33 people and injuring many more. A Gullop-institute checked public opinion and found out 55% of the Iraqis consider their situation and their prospects as "worse than under Saddam". The UN found an illegal prison north of Baghdad packed to brink with 620 prisoners; 16 of them deserved medical treatment because of torture they'd survived.

Huge explosions shattered East England when a petrol raffinery in Hamilhampstedt 70 was bombed;the explosions were heard on Sunday all accross England. 60 people were injured but there were no deads. Official reports said "the blast series were'n accissident, no terrorists' action".

****

02-11-2005

The Washington Post reported that CIA runs since 2001 series of secrete prisons abroad mostly in Thailand, Afghanistan & in a former East Block country-either hungry Romania, corrupt Bulgaria or Holland. There suspected al Qaida detainees were allegedly interrogated with no chance to confront their cases, with no human rights & with no court procedure. Thailand rejected the claims for protection its own tourist industry. But same night muslim riots cut electricity in a whole city in south Thailand. Red Cross speaker Antonella Lothari demanded Red Cross' immediate access to all undisclosed detention "centers" in 8 friendly countries. The US Secretary of State Dr. Condoleeza Rice denied the praxis known as

< RENDITION >:
prisoners's transfer into different countries for interrogations using the local law;but she rejected any claim of torture of prisoner, detainees and "illegal combatants": "Everything was in the frame of the international law, we use only lawful means in the battle against international terrorists in the strugle to defeat them fully & entirely, the CIA has not used third contries, their airspaces, their air fields, their prisons for interrogation", boasted Dr. Rice to the BBC diplomatic correspondent Johnathan Marcus on 05 December 2005. In fact CIA used massively chemicals & narcotics to destabalize'm mentally & to declare'm insane: "to make them soft & dizzy ":it is an old Dutch praxis widely used in Holland by its large prisons' network despite Holland's huge budget deficite. But Condoleeza Rice-doctor of law- denied any torture in CIA-prisons as "intolerable" and "USA respected national souveraignity of those countries not using them for interrogation by torture despite most of these fighters are stateless. We have to bring terrorists to justice!". After her statement she flew to Holland to discuss the <RENDITION> issue with Dutch prison officials. Holland runs a dense prison network despite its budget deficiency.

In Quetta the Pakistani forces managed to arrest a Syrian al Qaida fighter with $5,000,000 award on his head. The Pakistani President Pervez Musharraf revoked the purchase of 50 American fighter jets for the price of $40,000,000 each in order to boost maximally the eartquake relief. The help for Pakistan was harshly reduced compared with the Tzunami-help for Thailand and Indonesia which are tourism countries. But the BBC-specialist on Pakistan Liese Doucet commented on the Paris youth riots from the BBC studio in ....London.

In Kabul a bomb went off after suicide bomber ramed his car a US convoy. 15 marines were killed. The Pakistani news paper the "Dawn" announce the death of the al Qaida operative commander he died in the Pakistani gun fire.

****

01-15 January 2006

Iraqi liberation forces attacked 3 US patrols in Northern Baghdad and killed 6 US marines. The senior judge of the Saddam Hussein "trial" Amin resigned because of political, govermental & juridical mistakes. Nevertheless his "trial" will contionue in a "week". In Kerbala 50 people died in a funeral procession when a Suni militant suissider addressed his protest to the crowd of maurners. Iran railed the UN Security council for banning its nuclear program: "The Western countries did not restrict Israel from its nuclear program and encouraged Israel for its militant nuclear research program, despite the UN-non proliferation treaty"", Iran said and Saudi Arabian foreign minister Faysal al Saud confirmed.

More over minister Faysal accused the Western countries of helping & tolerating Israel of developing the atomic bomb; he stressed again "Saudi Arabia will not aim, strain, develope, produce or possess atomic weapns because is senceless!"

16 -31 Januari 2006

The senior judge of the Saddam Hussein Amin resigned because "of presserure from the government" and "instructions from the USA". In north-west Iraq the guerillas shot American helicopter on patrol. The 2 pilots died. And around Basra the Iranians arrested 8 Iraqi soldiers for oil smuggling. The 9th died during the arrest procedure. In Bayji a suicide bomber detonated him self during a funeral procession, killing or injuring ca. 100 people.

The judge of the Saddam Hussein trial retreated because "he was pressured by the government to make convinient decisions. In protest against the new judge al Rahman, 6 of Saddam's co-defendents and their lawyers didn't appear to court session on 01February 2006.

The French President Jacque Chirac declared "France will use its atomic weapons against any country which should commit terror attacks on France or French interests abroad". US President George W. Bush said "the situation in Iraq is very difficult, but we will continue with the peace process with no hesitation".

A Danish news paper and the Danish government apologized to Saudi Arabia "for publishing caricatures of the prophet Mohammed on its pages" and disclosed also other caricatures it had published on its web site. The Saudi government accepted the apologations. Saudi Arabia is the biggest oil producer & the biggest oil exporter in the world.

But the German news paper <Die Welt> approved the Danish move and published another caricature of the prophet Mohammed on its front page. The French news paper <François> approved the German publication. The Danish offices in Copenhagen were closed because of Muslim protests of Muslims. In Egypt & in Lebanon the Danish were attacked by angry Muslim protesters. 11 Arab countries declared a boykott on Danish, Norwegian Swedish milk products. After the boykott the Dans dismissed 110 workers from different milk & conserves industries. The Danish embassy in Beyrut & in Damascus were set afire by angry Muslim mobs while an Egyptian ferry was sanked in the Red Sea.

The Danish Prime minister Erasmus Ramussen apologized but could'nt prevent or stop the excesses surrounding the boykott of Egypt, Palestine, Jordan, India, Indonesia, Iran, Pakistan, New Zealand & even Afghanistan; the Danish Prime minister apologized repeatedly, but he couldn't change the course of such a hatred for the better. In Gaza the protests escaled but were kept under control after the Norwegian Embassy was set afire by angry mobs. Norway refused to apologized for the cartoons' published and demanded a compensation above all limits of shame. In fact Norway criticised Syria & Lebanon for failing to protect their diplomatic staff. Even in Afghanistan Norwegen troops in Minaman, Kabul and Kandahar were targetted and pelted with stones and rotten fruits. One protester was shot dead. Holland sent 1,400 troops to the region. An influencial Iranian news paper proposed to organize a competition for best caricaturs and cartoons on the haullocast

5-15 February 2006

An Egyption ferry sank in the Red Sea : 1,400passengers died. The rescue operations began too late.

The cause for the explosion and than for the sinking remained not clear.

At the same time the Caribbean state of Curaçao exported 2,000kg of cocain to Holland. The party arrived at the Dutch port of Rotterdam.

In the Red Sea a passingers' ferry sank to the bottom after a short explosion & fire on board. 1,400 people died in their journey from Saudi Arabia to Egypt. The premisses of the ship company < MF-98> in Sarafaga were ransacked, plundered and set afire by angry mobs of the victims' relatives.

Meanwhile the scandalous Danish cartoons enflamed new clashes and bomb attacks in the Babel Shaji district of Baghdad in which 4 people were killed. In Bengazi angry mobs of Lybians attacked the Italian consulate after the Italian Information & Culture Minister Roberto Kalderoli appeared on television in T-shirt decorated by the blasphamous Danish cartoons:10 Lybians died in the riot but managed to set afire the Italian consulate:its staff of 80 was evacuated by Lybian forces. After the carnage the minister Kalderoli resigned but said "he does not feel guilty about theDanish cartoons & about his T-shirt". The Italian Prime minister Sylvio Berlusconi haled his resignation; Lybia suspended its interior minister for excessive use of force. In the oil rich Niger delta the clashes against the prophet Mohamed caricatures were so severe that the Dutch oil company SHELL suspended all exports & all deliveries. So Europe was caught & blocked from two sides- one from Iraq-Iran and one from Nigeria which is very close to Europe. Only after the oil prices sky rocketed emergency commission started to discuss the situation in a search of solution which will be too little too late.

In Kanat in South Afghanistan angry mobs attacked the local American military base. The Americans opened fire at the crawd and killed 6 people. In Maynana and Kandahar the protests ended peacefully. In Herat Sunis killed 16 Shiites on a procession to mark the holly day Shura- the death of Imam Hussein, founder of Shiite branch of Islam.

The Australian government started investigation into the Australian wheat company AWB for paying huge bribes to Saddam Hussein in the1990ies. The President of AWB & Co. ltd Andrew Lindberg resigned because of the scandal but the company denied any wrong doing.

11-28 February 2006

The American Vice President Dick Cheney shot with 2 bullets 77 years old lawyer Henry Willingtone (Wittingtone) during a weekend hunt party in Texas. The victim survived but from shock and stress developed a heart infarct;the media made a chain of talk shows satirizing the Vice President-something unbelievable for us Europeans. After the scandal gained speed it became clear that Dick Chaney had no valid gun licence properly endorced.

In the Saddam Hussein trial the defendents entered the court room in underwear as sign of protest of their treatment and shouted loudly "Down with Bush! Down with America! Long live the Iraqi people!" Afterwards they left the court together with their lawyers foiling again any court negotiation.

In Aman the Jordanian supreme state court sentenced to death 9 al Qaida fighters, 4 of them in absencia The sentenced al Qaida militants shouted loudly to protest against the court decision calling Jordania "a stooge of America and Israel". Co-defendents al Zarqawi & al Shakhiri were absent continued to hide.

In Peshawar, in Karachi & in Islamabad mobs were rioting repeatedly against the publication of the cartoons insulting the Muslim prophet Mohamed in several European newspapers torching $100,000,000 worth of property:shops, banks, cinemas ... etc; 6 men died in the riots. Iranian news paper announced officially "competition of haullocaust caricatures using the same standards in freedom of speech as the Europeans". Holland closed "25,000 working places because of the expensive oil" but sent in 1,400 new troops.

A video footage was revealed in Amarra in Mayzan province showing British soldiers beating and kicking repeatedly Iraqi teen agers. Subsequantly the mayor of Basra and the city council refused any cooperation with the Brits: the next daythe mayor of Amarra followed suspending all contacts and all cooperation with the British and demanded the release of Iraqi prisoners from the British jails. The British admitted "they were progressively losing control on the south sector of Iraq and on the city of Basra which is the only Iraqi port.

Iranian foreign minister al Moutaki (deliberately pronounced as al Moussaka=Muslim patatoe meal) also required a fool retract of the 8,000 British troops in Iraq because "they were destabilizing the Gulf region beyond any control", said BBC.

The Al Arabia TV channel and an Australian television channel showed another 2-minutes video from the notorious Abu-Ghraib prison near Baghdad which documents abusing, beating, kicking and shooting dead Iraqi prisoners by the prison stuff. The victims were sprinkled with blood from beatings and shots. The video was shot in 2003. The US Defense Department speaker John Bellinger denounced the publication but admitted that "25 US military personal went on trial, were reprimanded or lowered in rank already". US Defense Secretary Donald Rumsfeld warned "there are more videos & photos to come...; " the Iraqi President Ibrahim al Jafari condemned the American praxis of cruelties. The UN published a report on the conditions in the Guantanamo concentration camp and said "the conditions there were absolutely inhumane and cruel esp. the fact detainees were kept in for four years without trial and accusations..... this treatment is aimed not to tame terrorism but to get intelligence information on al Qaida", admitted the White House spokesman Scott McLaren. But in fact the White House was furious at the report & strongly denounced it as" defaming to the UN, re-hashing & destructive" and asked the UN for an excuse which they didn't give on the issues "torture of detainees, beating them, keeping them in since years, intimidating them by military dogs in breach of all international laws and humanity standards"... etc. The UN Secretary General Kofi Annan praised the report and "asked Washington to close the camp, where some 500 prisoners were kept in without charge since years".

The Iraqi President Ibrahim al Jafari denounced strongly the recent attacks & assassinations of Suni activists by Shiite soldiers, police men & militias and launched an investigation in the matter after some 500 Sunis were killed by Iraqi police or Shiite soldiers in police uniforms. The news that the Sunis were attacked by Shiite police dead squads was met with hatred both in Europe and in the Muslim world. But Iran protest ed against the presense of 8,000 British troops in Iraq and asked for their immediate withdrawl: something which Iraqi people and the Muslim world demanded in order to stop the bloody Anglo-American oil war which cost over 100,000 Iraqi lives and was been blocking the world economy to grind down for years because of the expensive oil price. In Holland it cost 25,000 new unemployed for 2005. The Iraqis also said the British troops were destabilizing the region without any need. Teheran confirmed the claim. No numbers were anmnounced however about the victims from the both sides. A bit later 6 US marines were killed in south-east of Baghdad and 2 American helicopters were shot down or collided in mid-air in Jibutti:all 16 crew members died; some helicopters'chunks & 3 dead bodies were recovered by American, Dutch & British rescue teams. In Basra 2 contractor

Macedonian workers were kidnapped. The kidnappers demanded 100,000 USD ransom. The British admitted "they were progressively loosing control on the South Sector". Above all the deadly virus H5N1 causing bird flue (=influenca avione) spread in Iraq and even in France;the Iraqi oil minister admitted "the attacks on pipe lines & other oil facilities cost Iraq $60,000,000; there 165 such attacks for the year 2005", said a BBC correspondent from Iraq.

In Baghdad itself 3 suicide bombers detonated their devices in open area market killing 33 people.

Another 25 police were killed after a suicide bomber detonated himself at a police station "for special anti-terrorists' exercises". In eastern Baghdad a van was found with the bodies of 18 Shiites shot from a close range, probably executed. Another van was also found with bodies riddled by bullets;and in Baquba a valley was discovered with 50 decapitated bodies. The Shiite leader Moqtada al Sadr called "for mercyless attacks on Americans", after the Americans attacked a police station in Baghdad killing 18 people.

The American ambassador to London Mr. Tuttle was publically denounced by the Mayor Ken Livingstone "for acting as a little crook": allegedly ambassador Tuttle refused again to pay a small charge of 8 pounds equal to $13 in a time when American war in Iraq cost some $180,000 daily.

An American journalist of the Christian Science Monitor Jill Carol was released from Iraqi custody after've been kidnapped 3 months earlier. To the Press she declared: "I was treated extremely good in terms of food, water, showers, phone calls and now I celebrate my release". But the number of the ordinary Iraqis displaced by secterian violence the whole month of March rose to 30,000, said AP. The American Secretary of State Condoleeza Rice visited the town of Blackburn in North-West England but was booed and shouted at as a sign of protest;many parents let their children to stay away from school as a protest against the war in Iraq.

16 June 2006

The Jordanian militant Abul al Zarqawi was murdered by the Americans by a 200 kiloton TNT bomb on his house after a tip off. The third lawyer of Saddam Hussein & the former vice-president Barzan al Ramadan was murdered by American loyal troop. The barristers protested and demanded a better security. Security in Iraq?? Under the Americans?? The chief prosecutor demanded already their dead penalties.

In a Baghdad bus a planted bomb exploded killing 50 people & injuring 100 more.

****

A team of Russian doctors arrived subsequently in Holland to examine the body of Slobodan Milosevic: they said "he had not received a proper medication for his hart problems". His son Marko Milosevic said bluntly "he was poisoned". While the president Zdenko Tadic forbade any funeral in Serbia and ruled out any form of state funeral the prime minister Woislaw Kostunica declared just the opposite because he depends on the Socialist Party majority in the Parliament. The court itself abolished the arrest warrant of Mira Milosevic and invited her to come to Serbia provided that she'll surrender her passport on the boundary. Later on all restrictions were lifted and Kostunica declared "Milosevic will be burried at a national burial in Belgrade". 350,000 Serbians were estimated to attend his burrial. Meanwhile the results of the toxicological test were not announced on Tuesday as initially declared

****

16-01-2006

In Western Afghanistan an American helicopter was shot down by the liberation forces after several warnings. The helicopter crew died after. The Americans claimed themselves they killed al Qaida NR.2 al Zarhawi. In fact the world media showed the chared & maimed bodies of 18 women & children of a remote hamlet of the Uruz-ghan province. The Pakistani president Pervaze Musharaf protested at the American government for the senceless killing of weaponless civilians.

The CNN-channel was cut of from Iran for 24 hours after reporting mistakenly "Iran aims construction of atomic weapons" instead of "peaceful atomic technology". Iran accepted the CNN-apologation and resumed the CNN-broadcasting inside the country. In few weeks later Iran announced "continuation of its atomic research for peaceful aims".

****

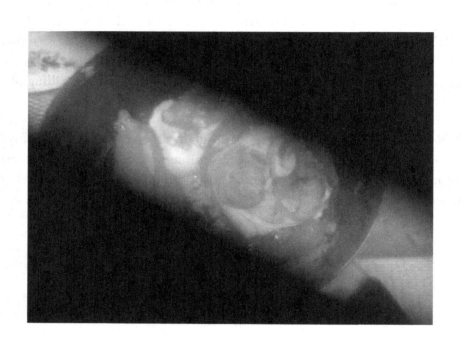

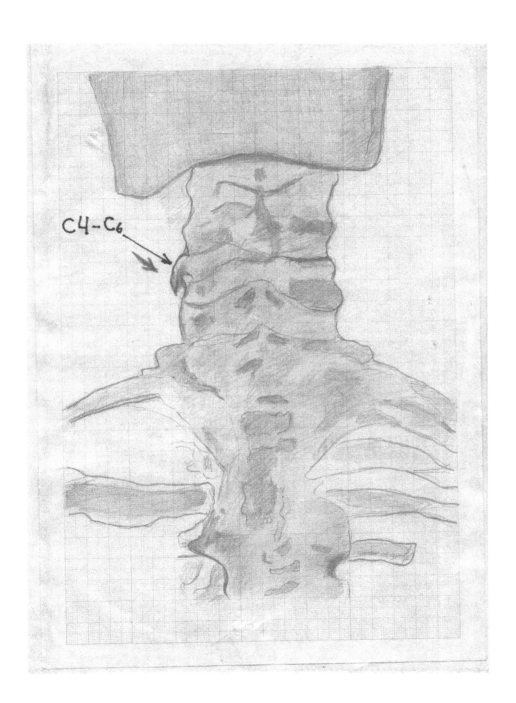

C4-C6

1O DOWNING STREET
LONDON SW1A 2AA

From the Direct Communications Unit   25 February 2004

Mr Emil Tzolov
219 Havekamp
The Hague NL-2592 BB
The Netherlands

Dear Mr Tzolov

The Prime Minister has asked me to thank you for your
recent letter and the enclosure.

Yours sincerely

STEVE AUST

AIR MAIL   0066556   LONDON 25.02.04 SW1   GREAT BRITAIN 0047 PB502244 POSTAGE PAID

Mr Emil Tzolov
219 Havekamp
The Hague NL-2592 BB
The Netherlands